WHOLESALE
101

A Guide to Product Sourcing
for Entrepreneurs and Small Business Owners

JASON A. PRESCOTT
WITH TARA GLADSTONE

New York   Chicago   San
Mexico City   Milan   New

1 2 3 4 5 6 7 8 9 0   QFR/QFR   1 9 8 7 6 5 4 3

ISBN   978-0-07-181136-1
MHID   0-07-181136-2

e-ISBN   978-0-07-181137-8
e-MHID 0-07-181137-0

Library of Congress Cataloging-in-Publication Data

Prescott, Jason.
    Wholesale 101 : a guide to product sourcing for entrepreneurs and small business owners / by Jason Prescott.
        pages cm
    Includes index.
    ISBN-13: 978-0-07-181136-1 (alk. paper)
    ISBN-10: 0-07-181136-2 (alk. paper)
        1. Wholesale trade. 2. Purchasing. I. Title.
        HF5420.P74 2013
        658.8'6—dc23   2013007851

To my mother, Iris. Mom, I love you so much. I can only hope that I am able to touch as many lives as you have. Thank you for the gift of life and blessings of love.

To my daughter, Deanna Rose; brothers, Jonathan and Justin; and best friend/CTO, Lester C. Hughes—my passion comes from you and burns for you.

11/11/2012

Contents

Introduction

SURVIVAL IS a basic instinct that has been ingrained in me since childhood. My father left my mother with four boys when I was nine years old. We grew up very poor and relied on food stamps for groceries and free meal passes for school lunches. Iris, my mother, worked 60 hours a week and went to school full time to finish her degree in nursing. While us boys were often busy getting into trouble and fending for ourselves, Iris was busy surviving. She didn't want anything to stop her from receiving an education. Her intention was to lift us out of our difficult circumstances. I ended up dropping out of high school and hopping around living at various friends' homes until one day I decided to get a GED and enroll in a local community college. The decision was simple—I wanted more out of life and realized that street smarts were only going to get me so far.

Then, in November 2000, I found out that in nine months I'd be a father. At the time, I was 23 years old, finishing up my B.S. in law administration at Western Connecticut State University. My experience in the professional world was pretty much limited to watching news clips on CNBC. Living in Fairfield County, Connecticut, where the main industries are financial services, information technology, and medical and chemical manufacturing, meant that the chances to learn about digital media, product sourcing, and global trade weren't easy to come by.

On a chilly morning in November, I had an interview at Sumner Communications, Inc., with Mr. Scott Sumner. Sumner Communications was a small business-to-business media publisher that owned the Merchandiser Group magazines, *Cover Magazine*, and Wholesalecentral.com. Scott was not impressed by my résumé. My credentials were limited to a few construction jobs and clerical duties at retail stores. He saw something else, though, that could not be reflected on a piece of paper.

My passion and drive to succeed were insatiable. During the interview, when all else seemed to be failing, I remember that my plea for being hired was that I was poor, smart, and hungry—both literally and metaphorically. Somehow the account-executive job that I was interviewing for became mine. I stayed with Sumner Communications until the end of 2004, when I joined another market incumbent for four months until starting JP Communications, Inc., in April 2005. Many people think that JP Communications stands for "Jason Prescott Communications" or, because I have two brothers in the company (Jonathan and Justin), that it was named for all the "JP" siblings. But the true story behind the name is that I founded the company with my partner at the time, Joseph Preston. Since both our initials were JP, JP Communications, Inc., seemed like the right choice.

While at Sumner Communications, I set many sales records. A few folks whom I know who still work there tell me that my records have not been surpassed. The nickname given to me around the office was the "Golden Child." Being the new kid on the block and the only business-development employee under age 30 certainly brought its pressure and stress to perform. Often I found myself making over 100 phone calls a day and averaging over three and a half hours of phone time. And there was rarely a day when I wasn't the first to arrive and the last to leave. If there was a commission to make, I wanted to make it.

My knowledge of import/export and the retail/wholesale industry was more than limited at that time—it was nonexistent. So how in the world did I obtain 30+ accounts per month, receive various promotions, take on duties that included print and web sales, and become the top financial earner at something I knew so little about? I found that enthusiasm was more than 50 percent of the sale. It was a contagious virus capable of turning the average Joe into a superstar money rainmaker.

I had enthusiasm not only for my daily job's duties but also for the industry. I picked apart every single magazine, piece of literature, web article, and person I could learn from. I didn't stop until my thirst for knowledge was fully quenched. The day Joseph Preston and I made the switch from being employees to entrepreneurs maximized the level of enthusiasm already bottled inside me. It was the first company I ever started, and now the responsibility of having to do more than generate enough sales to produce income for survival was paramount. I had to understand business operations, accounting, human resources, client services, and executive leadership. They all had to become high-level and equal priorities.

I'm still not sure how I fell in love with global trade in the first place, maybe because of my aspiration to achieve more and see the world, but knowing that what we do 24 hours a day enables global trade and entrepreneurialism is an amazing feeling. Since April 2005, when JP Communications, Inc., was founded, the company has had millions of users source, connect, and transact with thousands of suppliers all over the world.

As dynamic as global trade and product sourcing may be, the cornerstone of it all is great relationships and a passion to thrive in a world more connected than ever before. I've learned that being surrounded with great people and maintaining a passion with a constant drive to learn are the key ingredients to success. And this doesn't only apply to business but also to life.

Shortly after acquiring Manufacturer.com in early 2008, I truly learned the importance of relationships and what it meant to be a worldly person. At the end of 2010, Dominique, my fiancé at the time, and I moved to Hangzhou, China, to oversee a wholly owned foreign enterprise called Hangzhou Flat World Sourcing Media, Ltd. We hired dozens of developers and had these lofty plans to master China overnight. However, our plans hadn't taken into consideration one important and vital element to achieving success—culture.

This is why this book is not intended to be, nor is it, another self-published and self-proclaimed primer on how to master China. You need to live and work in China for years before you can fully understand the Chinese way of doing business. Any person who claims to have mastered

China without that experience or who claims to know all the secrets of global trade is not worth listening to. Besides, the bookshelves and Internet pages are already covered with self-published hoop-la on how to dance with government officials overseas and become a billionaire. We all know that's not how it's going to happen.

What this book *can* teach you, however, is how to use the various sourcing methods and resources out there to find the best wholesalers and manufacturers for your products. You will meet your business's goals by learning about trade shows, business-to-business (B2B) magazines, and B2B sourcing platforms, as well as how to find the appropriate suppliers (wholesalers, importers/exporters, and/or manufacturers) for you. Not only will this book teach you how to navigate through mega-international sourcing events at trade shows and walk you through the process of sourcing online, but it also will introduce you to other types of trading partners such as manufacturer's reps, trading companies, and suppliers that drop ship. Knowing how to work with these resources can help you to achieve success. You'll learn how to build solid relationships with all these partners and be given expert tips and strategies on sourcing the best products. You'll also learn about important business factors that have an impact on the net earnings of your business. I will give you expert and easy-to-follow advice because I was once in your shoes.

I encourage you to take the risk to be an entrepreneur as many who contributed to this book once did. Wayne Gretzky said, "You miss 100 percent of the shots you never take." JP Communications, Inc., took lots of blind shots the first few years when starting out. And it was through our toughest times, that my partner and I learned to be resourceful. Failure and success go hand in hand. Making mistakes and taking chances can only help you to move forward with more strength and wisdom.

This journey has lead to a destination more rewarding than I ever could have imagined. JP Communications, Inc., has now become the online B2B media partner of the most recognizable trade shows in the United States. It's thanks to great partners such as ASD, SOURCING at MAGIC, the National Hardware Show, the Off Price Show, and many others that I have had so many opportunities to contribute to small businesses and budding entrepreneurs.

Furthermore, trade continues to change. Around 2014 or 2015 there's going to be a massive shift in how the United States receives imports. The completed expansion of the Panama Canal is predicted to end the monopoly on import/export that West Coast ports have enjoyed for decades. Ports in New York, Houston, and New Orleans will create loads of new jobs, and they will have new locations for landing points and import offices. Megaships that once had to drop off the goods in the Long Beach ports (with an average lead time of three or more weeks to reach an East Coast destination) will now take no more than 14 to 16 days to arrive. When these new channels open for business, you can expect to see a significant increase in import/wholesale showrooms across the eastern seaboard of the United States. Within the next five to seven years, Los Angeles will have quite a bit of competition, and these monumental shifts will affect your business.

After reading this book, I hope that you will understand the importance of thinking and planning ahead as political agendas and global events affect your business. You need to pay attention to these factors, coupled with trade resources, relationships, and smart operational decisions, to achieve success. Throughout this book you'll learn why the bonds you form with the people with whom you work in business are just as important as the close bonds you've formed in your personal life.

This book will spark innovative thinking. Tara Gladstone, my research and writing assistant, and I have interviewed over 60 industry leaders and experienced veterans. We'll provide you with insider advice from these experts, including former top brass at Pepsi Worldwide, a senior manager at Walmart, executives from the Los Angeles mayor's office, and many other exciting and successful entrepreneurs. We got them to share their advice and experience. When you are done reading, you will be prepared for achieving not only wholesale sourcing and unique product manufacturing success but also entrepreneurial success.

I like to think that it's been seven years since my last day of work. My hobby and passion are connecting people and businesses, creating successful relationships, and facilitating creative thinking for the millions of people who have used my company's services over the last seven years. Thank you for giving me this opportunity to help you. May you enjoy your journey and achieve great success!

Acknowledgments

FIRST, I'D like to say a general thank you to all the businesses, organizations, and people who contributed content and research material to this book. I am very grateful for the insight, time, energy, and experience that you all provided. Product sourcing and global trade are only made possible through sharing experiences and forming trusting relationships. Without your support, this book wouldn't have been the same. May all your businesses experience great success in the years to come!

Next, I'd like to thank the people who were involved in the literal creation of this book. Tara Gladstone, this book would not have been possible without you. Your passion, dedication, and hard work made this project happen, and all the research and contributions you provided kept it moving in the right direction. You have an amazing career ahead of you, and I look forward to writing many more books with you. Brad and Deb Schepp, your consulting on this project also has been invaluable. I truly admire all the great books you have published in your career because they have helped so many uncover challenging technological topics. Writing my first book has been made possible only by assembling a world-class team of true experts and good people like you. May your editorial and publishing prowess continue to ignite the delight of readers. I look forward to tackling another project with you in the near future. Bill Gladstone, thank you for taking me under your wing. I remember you calling me "one of the good ones." Well, it takes "one of the good ones" to see the aspirations and intentions of another. You are a genuinely gifted thought leader, and thank you for making me a member of "the gang." And last but not least, Jennifer Ashkenazy, my editor from McGraw-Hill, thank you for your guidance and support throughout this project. I am grateful that McGraw-Hill saw the potential that this book has to offer.

Now I'd like to thank some specific people for contributing ideas, insights, and knowledge to this book. Let me start with the trade-show crowd. ASD, SOURCING at MAGIC, Internet Retailer, the National Hardware Show, and the Off Price Show are comprised of some of the most amazing people with whom I work. All my knowledge and experience in the trade-show industry is directly attributed to the special people with whom I've formed close relationships. Good partners are essential for the success of any business. I am forever grateful to all the executives and key players in this industry for the mutual trust and our strong working relationships that continue to thrive. I especially want to thank Chris McCabe, senior vice president of ASD Group; Camille Candella, marketing director of the ASD Group; John Banker, sales director of the ASD Group; Karalynn Sprouse, vice president of MAGIC; Steve Krogulski, CEO of the Off Price Show; David Lapidos, vice president of the Off Price Show; Ed Several, senior vice president of the National Hardware Show; and Molly Rogers, COO of Internet Retailer. You all hold the key to empowering so many businesses in our economy. May the growth of your shows continue, and thank you for all the support throughout our projects.

Roni Miller and the Fashion Institute of Design and Merchandising (FIDM), thank you for all the insight and resources that you have provided over the last six months. The FIDM is very lucky to have great educators like you, and there is no question that your teachings enlighten many. I look forward to working with you in the years to come, and I hope that together we will touch the lives of the students and businesses we seek to empower.

Alain Stambouli, you are one of the most intelligent human beings I know and a friend that I am dearly lucky to have. Watching the growth of Via Trading over the years has been more than impressive. You and your brother Jacques run a tight ship, and I wish nothing but success for every venture you pursue. Via Trading was one of my first customers, and I thank you for giving me the opportunity to be part of the story of our symbiotic growth. The ideas you have given me over the years continue to spark new products that millions of people benefit from using.

Thank you Michael Fan, CEO of New Times in Shenzhen. Finding business partners in global trade is one of the most daunting tasks. Together we have already accomplished some amazing feats as our companies continue to make the supply chain more transparent to navigate. The visions we share help to connect China and the United States in ways that power entrepreneurs and businesses to connect safely and securely. May our ideas continue to spark new trade, and may the initiatives that JP Communications, Inc., and New Times pursue be blessed with good fortune and success.

The China Chamber of Commerce for Import and Export of Textiles and Apparel (CCCT), especially directed by Mr. Wang Yu, has helped to open new doors for JP Communications, Inc. Thank you for your trust and commitment. The CCCT is a key player in the huge import and export industry and helps to stimulate global trade in monumental ways. The 12,000+ businesses that you serve in China are very fortunate to have your direction and insightful leadership. Thank you for giving me the opportunity to serve your members. May the projects we purse together benefit many and become an example of how partnerships among international organizations (especially from the United States and China) can flourish.

Jian, Keyin, Sandy, Mr. Gao, and Mr. Huang, the cultural experiences I've had with all of you have been invaluable. My ability to live, work, and do business in China has been made possible through our joining forces.

Joe, the name *JP Communications, Inc.*, wouldn't exist if you and I hadn't started this company together back in April 2005. Although we parted ways, I know that this company wouldn't have been started without you. Your technological genius and resourcefulness helped to make this dream come true. Thank you.

JP Communications, Inc., is also forever grateful to Roger Rappoport and the legal team at Procopio in San Diego. Your legal diligence has helped to steer the company safely down challenging paths. Roger, you are a great friend and the best darn business attorney I know. Thank you in more ways than I can express.

Jessica Wang, understanding all the challenging legal issues and corporate governance in China wouldn't have been possible without you. Your direction and guidance has helped me in countless ways. You are a truly gifted attorney and one of the most trusting people I have ever met. As our business grows in China, I look forward to receiving your direction, support, and friendship.

Claudia Bruemmer, you are such an angel. Thank you for all your contributions to *TopTenWholesale News* and for being part of everything I have done from day one. You are such a gifted writer and true editorial genius. Many people admire your wisdom, patience, maturity, and intelligence. To have a friend and colleague like you is more than a blessing. One day I hope that I can understand humanity as well as you do and develop the characteristics that have made you the amazing person you are.

Mr Scott Sumner, CEO of Sumner Communication INC, I thank you for hiring a poor, smart and hungry young man back in November of 2000. You were the best teacher and mentor that I ever had. Tough as nails and an intellect hard to parallel, your commitment to me helped mold a very successful entrepreneur. It is without question that you are a true business development genius who has gotten to where you are in business and life through leading with integrity and passion. Our relationship is dearly valued and I wish you nothing but fulfillment and success in all that you do.

Lester C. Hughes, you're one of the best friends and most talented technologists I know. Your leadership, innovative thinking, resourcefulness, and passion have provided my platform with a foundation that makes it all possible. Your technological innovations and resourcefulness amaze me every day. JP Communications, Inc., would not be possible without you. My employees, partners, customers, and users all embrace the foundation you've helped to construct. There isn't a day that goes by that I don't feel fortunate to be surrounded by your friendship and professionalism. As the best CTO and friend a person could ever ask for, thank you for inspiring me every day.

Jonathan and Justin Prescott, having two brothers like you by my side is such a blessing. The opportunities we have created together are not short of miraculous. Through the ups and downs, we have stood by each other's side and dedicated ourselves to what has become more than a passion. Attending countless trade shows, hammering away on the phones, and pounding the pavement has turned vision into reality. Throughout the last seven years we've accomplished so many amazing milestones. I love you both with all my heart and hope that our journey continues to offer blessings and a foundation for all. Thank you.

To Dominique Castro, our journeys together for almost six years were a guiding force to so much passion and inspiration. While living in the world together, our love for each other helped to create a foundation which shaped who I am today. Though the business at times consumed us, there could be no stronger testament that the spirit of entrepreneurialism is much more fulfilling when shared. May the next chapter in our lives provide a journey of fulfillment and give back to those we love.

1

The Changing World
of Product Sourcing

We are all working together, that's the secret.

—Sam Walton (1918–1992), founder of Walmart

To obtain success, retail and wholesale entrepreneurs need to know how to source products. Skip McGrath, online selling expert and coach, agrees, "As a retailer or wholesaler, you make money on products when you buy them, not when you sell them." That's why product sourcing is so important. In fact, knowing how to source successfully is one of the most closely guarded secrets among resellers. An eBay seller, for example, will share all kinds of information with new sellers just starting out; typically, they are that helpful. But just see what happens when you ask a seller where he sources his products from; he clams up.

Budding entrepreneurs, small businesses, and savvy traders become experts at sourcing by knowing where to research, how to communicate, and when to adapt throughout the process. This is why I have spoken to over 40 experts who share pointers and coveted advice about product souring that will help you to develop those skills. Designed primarily to

assist entrepreneurs, this book will provide you with practical information for

1. Finding and vetting domestic and international manufacturers
   or wholesalers
2. Searching for a factory to help turn your idea into a resalable
   product
3. Importing existing goods from overseas
4. Sourcing strategically using online business-to-business (B2B)
   trade platforms, trade shows, trade magazines, trading companies,
   manufacturers' reps, and other resources
5. Building strong relationships with trading partners

No matter which of the preceding you are trying to achieve, you'll
learn how to select and maintain healthy relationships with trustworthy
suppliers, which will enable you to achieve your business goals. You'll
also learn about all the benefits that different sourcing options offer
and why developing quality relationships with suppliers is the most
important thing you can do to obtain success in your retail, wholesale,
or trading business.

When people enter the world of product sourcing for the first time,
they often begin by focusing solely on the products. They want to find or
produce the least-expensive, best-selling products and don't think about
anything else. They forget about the fact that they will need to get those
products from people, namely, suppliers, whose business operations will
affect the success of their own businesses. Contrary to many a beginner's
perceptions, Mike Bellamy, founder and China operations director of
PassageMaker China, as well as the author of *The Essential Reference
Guide to China Sourcing*, clarifies that "the single most important factor
in determining the success or failure of your sourcing program will be
finding the right supplier."

I agree with Mike and would like to add that the only way to find
the best suppliers (and their stellar best-selling products) is by accessing
the right trade tools. To find those tools, you need to be up to date with

the technology and resources that have emerged, breaking the barriers to entering the B2B commerce-trading marketplace.

Evolution of the Sourcing Scene

While fundamentally product sourcing has never changed (it's still the act of finding products from wholesalers or manufacturers to resell through a business), technologically it's evolved into a whole new world. Not too long ago product sourcing was limited to word of mouth and archaic media for locating wholesalers and manufacturers. People used to have to literally go knocking on doors to find suppliers.

Jeremy Shepard, founder and CEO of Pearl Paradise, confirms this by sharing how his sourcing process has developed over the years:

> When I first started the company in the 90s, I had no idea about how to find sources. However, I was a flight attendant, so I could travel for free. I flew to locations all around the world where pearls were produced and pounded the pavement looking for suppliers. In Hong Kong (where pearls aren't produced, but there is a major trading hub), I went through the local phonebook and found companies that had the word *pearl* in their name and then went and knocked on their doors. Luckily, today things are much easier. We typically find new suppliers at the large jewelry trade shows in Hong Kong, which we attend three times a year.

This is just one example of many that I will share with you about how professionals have changed their sourcing tactics in recent years.

Evolution of Trade Shows and Business-to-Business Print Media

Over the last 10 to 15 years, sourcing online has revolutionized the way retailers and wholesalers source products. Going online to locate suppliers became much more common after September 11, 2001, when not only the world economy changed, but travel, hospitality, and many other sectors also went through rattling shifts. The national crisis that took place on that day made it less appealing for people to travel, which, coupled with the emergence of new digital media, technologies, social media, and ubiquitous high-speed Internet, forced trade shows to face some competition as business travel took a huge decline.

This led to a massive consolidation in the trade-show industry. The ASD trade show (formerly known as the Associated Surplus Dealers/ Association of Merchandise Dealers) used to have massive events in New York (at the Javits Center), Florida, Texas, and other areas. However, the company soon moved most of its shows to Las Vegas. And ASD was not the only major trade show to make these changes. Many trade shows that used to have smaller local shows now only had a couple of major events in one easy-to-access location.

Manufacturers and wholesalers also started to put their products online, and reselling professionals began flocking to the Internet to conduct all their industry research. Given these changes, the trade-show industry was cut by more than 40 percent in less than two years. The combination of the emergence of sourcing online and dwindling trade-show attendance made people fear that trade shows and business-to-business (B2B) print media eventually would disappear.

However, if you look at the sourcing industry today, this couldn't be further from the truth. The trade-show industry has not disappeared; things are just different. ASD's shows in New York are no longer the must-attend events for suppliers and buyers from all over the country. Today the company's events in Las Vegas are the most important, with an average of over 45,000 attendees and over 2,800 exhibitors. Also, trade shows are seeking expansion as the economy begins to resurge. ASD, for example, is currently planning to announce a new trade show in Miami beginning in 2013. The company wants to accommodate the increase in buyers and companies from the United States that want to export to South and Central America. This is an ideal location for language, culture, and ease of access. And other major shows, such as SOURCING at MAGIC, the Off Price Specialist Show, and the National Hardware Show continue to expand their international exhibits at a record pace. The Off Price

Specialist Show, for example, has seen its number of attendees grow by more than 25 percent over the last three years. In fact, it recently received an award for being the fastest-growing trade show (www.toptenwholesale. com/news/offprice-show-wins-fastest-growing-show-award-17207.html).

Trade shows also have incorporated technological advances such as blogger lounges and mobile technology that help buyers to get the most out of the shows. The trade-show industry keeps evolving, rather than becoming outdated, with rapid technological changes. Trade shows and B2B media have adapted with the ease that technology has brought to the sourcing industry and have, in turn, brought more valuable resources to global trade. And new shows have emerged to help you stay up to date with technological development. Shows that focus on e-commerce, such as the Internet Retailer Conference and Exhibition, have more than tripled in size over the last five years. I will be discussing more about all these exciting trade shows in Chapter 5, but for now, stay with me as I discuss B2B magazines.

The Enduring Business-to-Business Magazine Industry

Business-to-business (B2B) magazines also have continued to endure the changes in the sourcing landscape. Despite being the most traditional method of sourcing, trade magazines have many uses and are important tools in the retail and wholesale industry. One reason is their extra long shelf lives—the information in them stays relevant for a long time. Back when I first started selling print advertising in 2001, I would get dozens of callers a week renewing their subscriptions or requesting copies of editions from five years prior, which continues to happen today.

Scott Steele, publisher and CEO of *Canadian Merchandiser* magazine, confirms that B2B trade magazines are a popular method for product sourcing:

> From the retailer's standpoint, print trade publications are reli-
> able as they are something that you can hold in your hands. They
> represent somewhat of an authoritarian figurehead for buyers
> that you can utilize, not just for product sourcing, but also for the

editorial information that comes along with them. Retailers still like the idea of having a physical hands-on publication dedicated to their marketplace that gets delivered to them every month.

In addition, new magazines for the retail and wholesale industry have come into the mix to meet the demands of the technological changes taking place. Today there are magazines dedicated to retailers who sell online in the e-commerce industry.

Don Davis gave me a deeper understanding of how *Internet Retailer* magazine caters to the e-commerce industry:

> *Internet Retailer* magazine aims to provide retailers with information they can use to more effectively sell online. It's aimed at a wide range of online retailers, from the smallest seller on eBay, to Amazon and Walmart. It's designed to provide information for e-retailers of all types: those that sell only on the web, retail chains, manufacturers, and retailers that sell through catalogs and call centers. In every article, we try to answer the question: How can our readers make more money by reading this article?
>
> A small business or entrepreneur should subscribe to our magazines, visit our website, and use our research guides because they provide the most accurate and objective information and analysis about e-commerce. In each issue of the magazine we cover a range of topics, and each article is very specific. If you're interested in e-mail marketing or website performance, you'll find articles about those topics every few months in *Internet Retailer* and on our website. Those articles mainly quote retailers—not vendors—and provide reports from the front lines about how e-retailers are addressing these issues. Also, every article we've ever published, and that's thousands, is viewable on our website for free. Any retailer looking for information need only search our site for relevant articles. We also offer an e-mail newsletter, IRNewslink, which brings you breaking news on e-commerce five days a week.

Evolution of Business-to-Business Platforms

Business-to-business (B2B) trade platforms also have evolved considerably, even during their relatively short existence. What began as a simple Internet search engine, limited to listing suppliers' names, has now become your own personal sourcing assistant. Business-to-business platforms such as TopTenWholesale.com and Manufacturer.com enable you to send out product requests, look for verified suppliers, communicate with suppliers through instant chat tools, and use other resources that make managing your retail or wholesale business (and finding great suppliers) easier. In addition, the technological advances on B2B sourcing platforms make the supplier vetting process safer for buyers than ever before by verifying suppliers with the help of qualified third-party companies.

David Auren, an executive at Boulevard Apparel, explains how technological advances have improved his sourcing process:

> Before sourcing platforms such as TopTenWholesale.com came into the scene, I had to do a lot of legwork and visit a lot of trade shows. I still go to shows, especially to build quality relationships with suppliers, but sourcing platforms have made life so much easier. They've opened up channels of direct communication between buyers and sellers from the comfort of my own office. Now I don't have to travel as much, and I feel more comfortable when choosing suppliers that have been vetted for me by these platforms.

Technology and Product Sourcing

Through the use of the technological tools that we have access to today (which I'll describe in detail later on in this book), finding information about companies and communicating with them instantly are more achievable than ever before. This makes managing relationships with suppliers, even those located overseas, easier than ever before. The social media phenomenon has especially made it simple to vet and get to know suppliers. And this is just one of many tools available online today that help you to connect with suppliers. The Internet has provided the stage for momentous leaps in technology that have simplified the product sourcing process.

Megy Karydes, board member of the Fair Trade Federation and founder of www.World-Shoppe.com, agrees that product sourcing is more manageable than ever before:

> I started my business in 2004, and although it wasn't really that long ago, there weren't as many resources online for sourcing as there are today. Now technology has made it a lot easier to find great products from all over the world. We aren't restricted to going to trade shows or ordering from trade magazines.

The shrinking digital divide gives entrepreneurs worldwide the ability to start their own companies. Today millions of people run home-based businesses selling products through personal websites and sites such as eBay and Amazon. Product-syndication solutions (provided by companies such as Channel Advisor and Commerce Interface) have made it easy for resellers to market their products to hundreds of the largest e-commerce retailers through software and services that enable you to market and list products on multiple online venues.

With smart phones, tablets, and high-speed Internet connections, we are able to stay more connected than previous generations. Global trade is now as easy as entering a website address into your browser's search bar. Shipping logistic tools such as shipwire.com, online sourcing platforms such as TopTenWholesale.com, online accounting tools such as Quicken Online, and e-commerce website builders such as volussion. com make it simple for entrepreneurs to inexpensively set up a successful business and enter the market.

Starting your own business is now much more feasible than ever before. Today there are fewer restrictions on who can start their own business and achieve success. As Dominique Castro, cofounder of Twistlets (a fashion-accessory company for tween girls), explains, "It's a matter of starting with a vision and then following through with the right tools and research."

Importance of Research for Sourcing

One of the most important things you can do as an entrepreneur is research innovative trends and tactics. For product sourcing purposes, the best tools to use (and the ones that will help you to meet the best suppliers) include online B2B trade platforms, trade shows, and B2B trade magazines. If you go into the business without understanding these resources, then your chances of becoming the next Sam Walton should be exchanged for a lottery ticket.

Don't be concerned if you already have a business and have not yet mastered these tools. It's never too late to learn. Once you are finished reading this book, you will have a knowledge advantage over many of your peers. Lots of people in this business are not savvy about the latest technology and resources. And they certainly don't have all the information and tips that I am about to give you. You, on the other hand, are in a good place because you are seeking out the right resources.

Scott Steele, publisher and CEO of *Canadian Merchandiser* magazine, confirms that doing research will put you in a great position to enter this business:

> When you start your own company you will run into difficult situations and areas of business that you haven't dealt with before. Seeking out the right information (from the right people) is a means of support that can help you navigate through the tough times, and achieve multifaceted rewards further down the road. You will eventually have more control of your own destiny and life. Initially, your new venture is your entire life, and it needs to be viewed and worked that way.

I suggest that you still make time for your friends, partners, kids (if you have them), or whoever the folks are at home. Balance is important! But for the first few years especially, entrepreneurs will need to invest a great deal of time in their businesses. The more prepared you are, the better chance you will have to succeed.

In addition, research is important because as the sourcing industry's landscape is constantly changing, you too need to be up to date and evolve with changes to achieve success. You need to know about the innovative services available in the sourcing world today, such as international sourcing pavilions and VIP buyers' concierges at trade shows, articles updated daily on the web that share industry trends from B2B magazine companies, and the ability to place requests for quotations (RFQs) with hundreds of suppliers with the simple click of a button on a B2B trade platform. You also need to understand why it's important to source by using more than one approach. It's important to combine various sourcing methods and access all the opportunities that exist within various channels. Furthermore, you need to be aware of how globalization has made the world smaller than ever before. Now you can source from such places as Korea, Pakistan, and India, which gives you more options than ever before.

The Entrepreneurial Attitude

Before I get into specifics about the resources available for product sourcing, let me speak a little about the secrets that will make you a successful entrepreneur and a good businessperson in the wholesale and retail industry. After running a boot-strapped business for the last eight years as CEO of JP Communications, Inc., I have found that successful entrepreneurs share common traits that have helped them triumph. My discussions with entrepreneurs and industry executives for this book also confirmed my findings. They were once in your shoes and have made it as far as they have with the help of these traits.

One of the most important traits of successful entrepreneurs is that they live with passion and enjoy what they do almost every day. They have learned how to look forward to change and see the opportunities (not the obstacles) that surround them. They are always up for exploring innovative new practices in their industry, and they are confident and enthusiastic about what they do. Their enthusiasm is so contagious that it spreads to those around them.

• • •

To achieve this type of attitude, Cindy Teasdale McGowan, owner of Makaboo Personalized Gifts, advises the following:

Having a mantra. My mantra the last couple of years was, "Go BOSH—go big or stay home." I always have a mantra because it helps me stay focused, positive, and achieve success.

Entrepreneurs also know how to manage their money wisely. They create a budget, noting all their expenses, and they ensure that they don't go over this budget, especially when starting out. Marc Joseph, CEO and president of DollarDays International, Inc., explains why he suggests that you have enough money to last six months before you start your business.

Make sure you have enough money to last you for six months. No matter how smart you are, or how great you think that your business will be, people don't just rush in the moment you open your doors. That's something you are going to need to build up to. You've got to be able to market yourself and get the message out about what you are doing. That's why I highly recommend saving up enough money to pay your bills for the first six months.

There are a lot of costs involved in a retail and wholesale business. Knowing your budget will help you to plan and make better decisions. Don't be afraid to look at the numbers; anyone can start a retail or wholesale business, even on a tight budget. You just need to proceed strategically with a plan of where it's wisest to invest.

This leads into my next point—planning. You need to have a clear idea about what you are trying to create. Creating a plan with details about what you are trying to achieve will enable you to see your vision more clearly. The more clearly you understand your vision, the higher is the likelihood that you will bring it to fruition. However, don't get caught up in the planning phase. You don't want to spend so much time researching, discussing, writing, and honing the plan that you never get around to executing it! As Nikhil Jain, CEO of OnGreen, encourages, "Don't think too much about starting it. Just do it!"

You also need to project an image of professionalism. When you don't have a lot of experience, you have to improvise. You don't know exactly what you are doing because you have never done it before. But guess what, neither had anyone else the first time they started a business. Talia Goldfarb, cofounder of Myself Belts, explains why you don't need a ton of experience to make your dream become a reality.

First-time entrepreneurs need to know that they can do this. I would have been scared if I had thought about it too much. In my case, the ball started rolling, and I didn't have to make a conscious choice to take a step off the cliff. Experience isn't everything. You have to be open, hardworking, and talk to the right people. This will help you gain information and knowledge. You can learn a whole new industry; you just need to do it one day at a time.

You are closer to being a professional than you think. Already you've proven your seriousness by picking up this book. You just need to remember the simple things such as showing up on time, being helpful to your partners, taking your profession seriously (but not too seriously), having good communication skills, and staying focused on your goals. These things are not hard to do, but they make a huge difference in other peoples' perceptions of you. Maintaining a professional attitude will help you to stand out among your peers more than you can imagine.

You also need to promote yourself and your business. This is something that most people find a little tough in the beginning. It's always easier to speak highly about your partner's, best friend's, or sibling's talents than it is to speak about your own. But it's time to take yourself out of the shadows and show others how much you shine. It's okay to boast about the great job that your company is doing so that you can transmit the quality of your services to others. Get out there, tell people what you are doing, and say it with pride. Today there are so many channels for promotion. Social media, websites, trade shows, and B2B trade platforms are just a few that you can use. I'll be sharing many ways to market yourself and your business throughout this book, so don't worry if you don't know where to start.

You also need to know how to create a competitive advantage. What makes your company unique and stand out from the others out there? What added benefits will your company (or does it already) provide? A benefit can be as simple as great customer service or the most competitive prices. You just have to be sure to do what you promise (and do it well). As Jack Welch, former CEO of General Electric, says, "Bring out the three old warhorses of competition—cost, quality, and service—and drive them to new levels, making every person in the organization see them for what they are, a matter of survival."

• • •

Skip McGrath, online selling expert and coach, explained how one of his competitive advantages is customer service:

> My wife and I are in the business together, and we take customer service very seriously. One time a woman in Florida ordered a bottle of vegetarian Worcestershire sauce from us but received a bottle of Louisiana pepper sauce instead. When she got the pepper sauce by mistake, she returned it, and e-mailed me saying that she really needed two bottles of the vegetarian Worcestershire sauce as soon as possible. She needed it for a recipe for a party she was hosting that coming Saturday. So we immediately sent out the order again, and she received the pepper sauce *again*. It was at that point that we realized that Amazon had mixed up the two sauces on the shelves. On realizing this, I drove down to the Worcestershire sauce distributors' office (which was about an hour away from my house), got two bottles of the Worcestershire sauce, and sent it to our client with overnight shipping.
>
> I would have to sell thirty bottles of sauce to recover the cost on that transaction. But that is what you do. She gave us a glowing feedback, is really grateful for what we did, and wants to buy

more products from us. We go to great lengths to provide great customer service. That's why I am a top-rated seller with 100 percent good feedback on eBay and Amazon. In the end it pays off.

Skip is a perfect example of why you need to do your best and know what your competitive advantage is going to be. If you don't know what it is or how to provide it to your customers, someone else will.

Another habit that entrepreneurs have instilled in themselves is staying involved and participating in their industry. This is something that I will highlight and discuss throughout various chapters of this book. It's something that you need to master to achieve success in the retail and wholesale business. For now, you can start brainstorming about ways to reach your goals from the comfort of your own home. Here's a hint— social media is a great place to start.

Learning how to negotiate well is also an important skill. You can't always expect to get exactly what you want from the outset, so you need to be well versed in how to arrive at a win-win situation with your suppliers. You don't want to come across as overly shrewd and selfish, but you also shouldn't always be the first to fold. You need to know how to find that happy medium. I will give you some tactics on how to negotiate and help you to find the right balance with your suppliers and trading partners.

The last skill that is important to highlight when speaking about becoming an entrepreneur is seeking new and innovative ideas and practices for your company. The best way to spark ideas is by reading lots of varied materials and staying connected to other professionals. I will be getting into the details of how and where to do this soon, but it's good to know that the more connected you are to the pulse of the industry, the more inspired you will be. This will keep your business on the cutting edge and be of value to your customers.

Going for It

I urge you to stay enthusiastic as you look ahead to the exciting adventure on which you are about to embark. Yes, there will be tough times and hard work involved, but when you find the right suppliers and your

TRAITS OF SUCCESS

Jim Kozlowski, who worked at PepsiCo for over 20 years and retired as senior vice president and chief procurement officer, explained some of the traits that he believes make for successful entrepreneurs. Here are some of the ideas and attributes that he suggests are important for achieving success:

- Set a clear vision of the journey you are about to take.
- Always show eternal optimism with a contagious positive attitude.
- Be fearless and unafraid of failure.
- Exhibit passion, perseverance, and persistence at all times.
- Push the limits of intellectual curiosity.
- Be a good listener.
- Have the ability to see difficult times as challenges, not problems.
- In stressful times, be extremely focused and steady to get out of the situation.
- Always exhibit humble confidence and guard against arrogance.
- Realize that your success is a marathon race, not a wind sprint.
- Coach and support your people and realize that they are your most important resource.

business is thriving, you will feel a guaranteed sense of satisfaction. The pleasure that your venture brings will leave you with that beaming glow that makes others want to know what you have been up to.

David Stankunas, founder and CEO of Beard Head, Inc., also encourages you to let go of fear and take the plunge:

Just go for it; it's a lot easier than you think. I started my first company, Poker Bling, having had no experience creating an e-commerce website or sourcing anything from overseas. I had been entrepreneurial but had not yet experienced success. It was a bit of a leap of faith when I started. I spent $6,000 or $8,000 to get my first full production of the product made, and I had no idea if it would sell. Then I started doing lots of trade shows and experiencing success. I eventually sold that company, started my new company, Beard Head, Inc., in a similar way, and am now more successful than ever.

Conclusion

As you can see, many entrepreneurs once stood where you are today, with very little experience in product sourcing. You are going to be a giant step ahead of where they once were, which puts you in an even better position to achieve success. I hope that you feel encouraged to start your retail or wholesale business. Remember, the infrastructure that technology and globalization have created for you makes product sourcing easier than ever before. I also hope that you are excited about learning all the insider tips provided throughout this book. With these strategies—and the right mentality—you will be well on your way to victory. Get ready to become a sourcing pro!

Looking Ahead

Before you are ready to jump into the specifics of trade shows, print media, and B2B platforms such as TopTenWholesale.com, you first need to understand why it's so important to combine various methods and "step out of the silo." I want to help you leave your comfort zone to increase your chances for success in product sourcing. You'll learn the value in leaving no stone unturned when looking for suppliers and how using valuable business resources and information is an essential part of the sourcing process.

2

Stepping Out of the Silo

Keep away from people who try to belittle your ambitions.
Small people always do that, but the really great make you feel
that you, too, can become great.

—*Mark Twain (1835–1910), American humorist,*
essayist, novelist

I N CHAPTER 1 you learned how product sourcing has evolved from a reliance on word of mouth and print media for locating wholesalers and manufacturers to the emergence of trade shows and online business-to-business (B2B) trade platforms such as TopTenWholesale. com and Manufacturer.com. You also learned about what it takes to be an entrepreneur and how important it is to stay up to date with changes in the sourcing industry.

Some people begin with a specific method for sourcing and never expand beyond that approach. For example, a small storeowner may only feel comfortable looking at trade magazines because that is the way she has always done her sourcing. Unfortunately, sticking with only one approach limits her chance for success because she is ignoring all the suppliers and learning opportunities provided by trade shows and reputable online sourcing portals.

Limiting yourself to only one source of information is like being trapped inside a silo of your own making. The word *silo* literally means "a pit to hold grains." When your business is stuck in a silo, you are accepting the status quo and have stopped looking for ways to evolve. You let your competition charge ahead of you while you are stuck with a company lacking in innovation. Sometimes this happens because of the fear of trying something new or the lack of understanding of what to do.

But this doesn't have to be you. Using more options leads to smart and successful sourcing, which is the best way to control your price, supplier diversification, competitive advantage, and risk management. This is why I am going to show you how to ease out of your comfort zone with the vast amount of resources out there. By the end of this chapter you will be aware of how to gain more industry knowledge and explore new opportunities. You will grow accustomed to analyzing how others have grown their businesses and stepped out of the silo, and you will feel empowered to do the same.

A person's approach to sourcing becomes trapped in a silo when he or she

- Buys from the same suppliers without seeking new trading partners
- Attends only one event repeatedly
- Uses the same B2B platforms everyday
- Subscribes to the same trade publications without diversifying
- Reads only one source of news
- Avoids new technology
- Advertises in the same places every month
- Limits himself or herself to sourcing through one method (e.g., only using trade magazines to select new products or only using trade shows to look for new sourcing partners)

These habits are often attributed to a business that needs to branch out, change methods for finding information, and explore new sourcing resources. Getting trapped in the repetitive cycle of product sourcing in the same way every time will not lead to the best results for your business. What's right for your business today may not be what's right for it tomorrow; staying up to date with the latest sourcing and industry information will help you to ensure that you are always making the best decisions for your business. By discovering new resources and combining various sourcing methods, you will have a competitive advantage. You will have access to all available products and suppliers. There isn't one surefire combination for success. But with the tips and advice I am about to give you, including pointers from experts who have been down the road on which you're embarking, you will soon find the combination that works best for your business.

Using Social Media, News, Events, and Other Resources to Stay on Top of the Sourcing Game

Staying connected and participating with other people in your industry helps you to learn the ins and outs when you are just starting and keeps you abreast of important happenings no matter what stage you are in. It also keeps your mind active with innovative ideas for your business. Knowledge about your particular field and the sourcing industry in general helps you to make more educated decisions when looking for suppliers. Furthermore, your business has a better chance of obtaining success if you surround yourself with industry experts. Once you have built a successful business ecosystem around you, inspiration and ways of adapting your business strategies will come more naturally.

Valuable information and tools help your ecosystem to flourish and become more productive. Social media channels such as LinkedIn, Twitter, Facebook, Pinterest, Instagram, and YouTube, as well as business mixers, seminars, and events, are all great places to start. They allow you to join conversations, discover new business and product trends, and learn from experts who are veterans in the industry. Lisa Gleeson, founder and owner of Lisa's Gift Wrappers, is a big believer in the importance of using social media channels for your business. "I have five websites, an iPhone app, Constant Contact (for newsletters), Facebook, Pinterest, Flickr, YouTube, and LinkedIn. You have to use everything these days because it helps you to learn how to appeal to all ages and interests." By staying active online, you engage with people who share your interests and have the most up-to-date information about your field.

It ensures that your company evolves with the market. And knowing when it's time to change and/or expand is a key to success. Now let's look at how these tools help to generate ideas for expanding your supplier and product base.

LinkedIn

LinkedIn is a great tool for networking and obtaining information. If you do not have a LinkedIn account, I recommend that you create one as soon as you are done reading this section. For those of you who have an account but haven't updated it lately, I recommend that you do so as soon as possible. You should always keep everything on your profile accurate and current because it helps your trading partners (and customers) to evaluate your professionalism. If you look at the "Who's Viewed Your Profile?" section (located on the sidebar to the right-hand side of the site), you may be surprised by how many people have viewed your profile and how many times you have shown up in search results. With this in mind, it's important to represent yourself in the best way possible. You don't want to miss any opportunities that this network could provide. Dominique Castro, cofounder of Twistlets, a fashion-accessory company for tween girls, attests to LinkedIn's usefulness: "LinkedIn was extremely helpful with making buying contacts for my business. It helped me find the right people to achieve success."

LinkedIn helps you to find people within its community through features such as Groups and Answers. Groups are a great way to look for suppliers and industry peers (Figure 2-1). There are groups based on interests (both general and specific) for everything from merchandise to sourcing. Joining and participating in groups can lead to building quality relationships with sourcing partners and potential customers. You also will stay up to date on the topics and events that these groups are discussing. It's easy to search for groups that match your interests, and LinkedIn even recommends groups that you can join based on your profile and connections. I recommend joining the LinkedIn groups for ASD, SOURCING at MAGIC, the National Hardware Show, Off Price, and TopTenWholesale.

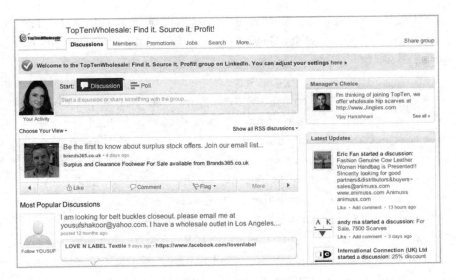

Figure 2-1 LinkedIn's groups can help you to meet suppliers and industry peers.

The Answers section on LinkedIn is helpful for finding solutions to problems or concerns related to almost any aspect of your business. You use this feature by posting a question and choosing the industry or business category to which it's related. Your query is then sent to other LinkedIn professionals from within the industry or category that you specified. The question is normally open for about a week, and as professionals respond, you receive e-mails with their answers. You also can go back to your own Q&A area in the Answers section and review responses at any time. This tool gives you a great chance to meet and learn from other people who are willing to help you through your business challenges. You can ask anything from "What trade shows should I attend?" to "What accounting system is best for a retail business?" Depending on the relevance of the answers you receive, you may want to connect with people who answer your questions. This is a great way to meet experts in your field. Furthermore, the Answer feature lets you browse questions that other professionals have already asked. You may find that your question has been asked recently and that the information you need is right there.

For those of you who feel shy about asking questions, Talia Goldfarb, cofounder of Myself Belts, sheds light on why asking them is actually a sign of intelligence:

> Sometimes people think that asking questions is a sign of weakness rather than a sign of intelligence. I've never looked at it like that because seeking out the right answer is the way to go. I remember that when I first started my business, I heard the term *FOB*, and I didn't know what it meant. I asked someone, and when she told me that it meant "free on board," I felt really silly. But if I hadn't asked her, I would have been proceeding with something that I didn't understand. Realizing what you don't know and seeking the answers out is much smarter than acting like you know information that you don't.

Talia now runs a successful company and has progressed from answer seeker to advice giver right here in this book. Remember, we all begin in the same place. We have to seek industry knowledge by asking questions of those more experienced than ourselves. Asking questions eventually will enable you to help others who were once in your position. Moreover, asking and answering questions can help to build credibility among your peers—it shows hunger for information and an ability to share expertise.

Twitter

The next tool that I am going to discuss is Twitter. This is more than just a place for sharing bursts of information or microblogging. There's a lot of power to be harnessed from this social network (Figure 2-2). Daria Steigman, founder and Communications Strategist at Steigman Communications, shares how Twitter has been helpful for her business:

> Twitter's biggest business value is often underappreciated—and that is building out your network and community of colleagues

and peers. That in and of itself has business development and professional development implications. Two examples of how Twitter helped me include

1. I connected initially via Twitter with someone who is now my business partner in a new venture.

2. My presence on Twitter and my contacts there have resulted in speaking opportunities at conferences.

Figure 2-2 Twitter can help you to find important information related to your industry.

One specific way to use this social media platform is by setting up Twitter Lists. Twitter Lists allow you to create an easily accessible group of select Twitter users. First, you choose Twitter members to add to the list. Then you are able to both send out tweets to everyone on the list (by using the Mentioning feature of Twitter) and see the content that members of the list generate (by looking at the list's timeline). I suggest setting up separate lists for suppliers, colleagues, competitors, customers, and any other group that you may find relevant to your business. This allows you to create tweets tailored to each group and/or follow only the tweets being created by members of the group. This also allows you to alert customers about special deals and find out what they are interested in. You can also use Lists to learn about new trends and see how your competitors are promoting themselves. This helps to generate new marketing or sourcing ideas and helps to ensure that you are not lagging behind on industry trends. Setting up Lists on Twitter helps you to stay organized and easily target the groups with which you want to interact. To find out more about how to use Twitter Lists, go to https://support .twitter.com/articles/76460-how-to-use-twitter-lists.

Another way to use Twitter is to search for information through hashtags or by trending topics. Twitter's Help Center explains that hashtags are keywords that have been denoted by the "#" symbol in a Tweet. People use hashtags to categorize the information they produce and make it more searchable. I suggest that you do a search for hashtag keywords that are relevant to your industry. For example, if you are in the women's apparel industry and want to know what the hottest new trends for the upcoming season are, search for something like "#fashiontrends," and you will be amazed by the quantity of information that comes up. Additionally, you can use hashtags to find a community that is interested in the same topics as you. Enter a search term with a hashtag such as "#trade shows," "#closeouts," or "#cantonfair," and find people who discuss the topic. This can help you to grow your network and meet potential customers or suppliers.

Also useful are Twitter's Trending Topics. Trending Topics are subjects that are algorithmically determined as the most popular on Twitter at the moment of the search. You can see these subjects listed on the left-hand side of the screen under "Trends." Twitter will tailor these Trending Topics to the people you follow and your location. If you are following relevant people and sources in your industry, this is a useful tool. You also can customize your settings if you find that the trends appearing in your feed are not from your geographic location or are about topics that do not appeal to you. To learn more about Trending Topics and how to use them, check out Twitter's "FAQs about Twitter's Trends" in the Features section of the Help Center.

TIP

Although originally created and intended for public relations and marketing professionals, Edelman's TweetLevel also may be useful for you. This tool helps you to find the most influential tweeters by topic. It measures the relevance of tweeters by how much influence they have in Twitter's community. It also allows you to see who influences these users and on whom they have influence. Looking at this information shows you who the important players in your industry are and gives you the ability to see what they are discussing. You can search on TweetLevel by entering a hashtag topic/keyword or a user's Twitter handle. I recommend that you start by searching for hashtag topics relevant to your business. Then see who the most influential tweeters are and follow them. To find out more and start using this tool, go to http://tweetlevel.edelman.com/.

Lastly, let's not forget about using Twitter when you are at an event or trade show. Personally, I love using Twitter at trade shows. The number of users tweeting from events such as the ASD, The Specialist Off Price Trade Show, and SOURCING at MAGIC, has grown significantly over the last two years. Find out what the trade show is using as its hashtag for the event, and you will learn important information about suppliers, events, and more.

Facebook

Facebook is another helpful tool for businesses. It allows you to search for Facebook pages, or public profiles, that share business interests and products with other Facebook users. By looking at a business's page, you can see what it is talking about, the new products it is working on, and how other people engage with the company. You also can search for Facebook groups or pages where groups of people can communicate about shared interests. Searching for any term from "Chinese suppliers" to "paper cups" will show you various groups within the Facebook community.

When doing a search, click on "All Results" (in the bottom of the search window), and you will see pages, groups, posts from your friends, applications, and web results related to the topic. Browsing the information from these various sources is helpful for seeing which product and sourcing trends are relevant to your peers and/or people who could become potential customers.

In addition to following pages and groups created by others, Facebook can assist you in getting the word out about your own company. By creating a Facebook fan page, you can feature your store's products, and people from all over the world can see them. Shreyans Parekh, cofounder of Koyal Wholesale, explains how Facebook has helped his company to achieve success:

> Social media has been tremendous for us in terms of sourcing new products and for leveraging our network. On Facebook alone we have over 15,000 followers that we are able to tap into on a daily basis for new product inspiration. We usually post images and "do-it-yourself" tutorial videos once we get product samples in. This allows us to test out the market and see if the product is right for our customers. As we receive feedback from the people who like our Facebook page, we are able to see if the product is following the trends or if it's a trendsetter in its own right.

Pinterest

Shreyans Parekh also uses Pinterest, a popular photo-sharing platform online. "With over 3,000 followers, we use Pinterest to test out colors, styles, sizes, and products in different tablescapes to see if they jive with other products of ours." Pinterest allows you to "pin" (or upload) pictures onto a virtual pinboard. You can display pictures of products that you are considering sourcing or that you already have in your store. The photos that you pin can be your own or photos that you find on the web. You can even create pinboards on Pinterest that act as catalogues. You can name a pinboard "Spring Collection" and post the entire collection of products on the board. If other Pinterest users like the product in one of the photos you have pinned, they can "repin" it (on their own pinboard), "like" it, or comment on it.

Monitoring which photos people like or repin can help you to learn about important trends and see what products potential customers are interested in. Furthermore, posting photos can drive traffic to your website. In fact, Mashable, a popular Internet news blog, has even published studies that show that Pinterest is driving more traffic to websites than Google+, LinkedIn, and YouTube combined (http://mashable .com/2012/02/14/pinterest-daily-users-are-up-125-percent/).

When using Pinterest, you should interact with other people's content as well. Repining other users' photos helps you to engage with potential customers. If you like or repin an item that someone else has posted, it helps users to understand your tastes and preferences and gives them an idea of the type of products they'll find in your store. And looking at other users' pinboards can help you to see what's becoming popular in stores similar to yours.

Pinterest is also a great tool for sourcing inspiration and investigation. You can look at trade-show companies' pinboards to find out what products and trends will be featured at upcoming shows. SOURCING at MAGIC uses Pinterest. The company has pinboards showing booths, runway shows, dresses, and more. Looking at trade shows' boards can help you to determine whether the trade show caters to your needs.

To learn more about the mechanics of using this platform, check out Pinterest's Help page (http://pinterest.com/about/help/). And to learn more about the ways to use Pinterest for marketing purposes, check out Mitt Ray's article, "6 Tips for Using Pinterest for Business," on Social Media Examiner (www.socialmediaexaminer.com/ using-pinterest-for-business/).

Instagram

Instagram is another fun, fast, and attractive way to showcase products and reach out to new customers. Through the use of a smart phone, you take photos and share them with the Instagram community. After posting photos on Instagram, you can also quickly share them on Facebook and Twitter.

Your main goal on Instagram is to generate a lot of "followers," or people who follow the pictures you post. An Instagram follower is like a Facebook "friend." When other users choose to follow you, your pictures appear on their Instagram homepage feed. Having a large following on Instagram helps to ensure that more people see your products and find out about your business.

You can help people find your photos by posting comments under them with hashtag (#) keywords. (Hashtags are used the same way as on Twitter, which I described earlier in the "Twitter" section.) Using hashtags allows Instagram users to discover your photos when searching with the Instagram Explore feature. The Explore feature also can help you to search for keywords about trends and sourcing-related information.

It's important that other Instagram users like/follow your photos because it helps you to reach out to new customers. The Following feature on Instagram shows users the photos their friends like or comment on. It also shows users which Instagram members their friends are following, which could help you to pick up new customers. When a member "likes" your photo or follows you, her followers see your name or your photo in their Following news feed (or the news feed that shows who her friends are following). If a person thinks your photo is interesting, it's likely that she will start following you too, which leads to the discovery of your company by new customers.

This photo-sharing platform can help you to become closer to the everyday lives of your customers. It's a great form of *guerilla marketing* (or marketing in a low-cost unconventional way). You also can use it to discover new trends, get product or marketing inspiration, and look at community reactions to see if a product you want to buy will be a good seller.

Shreyans Parekh explains how he uses Instagram for Koyal Wholesale:

Instagram is another photo-sharing platform that we use. We are advocates of this platform because it follows the theme of being visual. It is accommodating to our brides, caterers, and corporate clients who want to see products in their lifestyle setting. It has also been popular for developing a customer base and getting instantaneous feedback on products.

To find out more about how to use Instagram, go to http://insta gram.com/. And for more Instagram marketing ideas, check out Aleksandar Atanasov's article, "8 Tips for Marketing Your Business on Instagram," on Social Media Today (http://socialmediatoday.com/ aleks-atanasov/981386/8-tips-marketing-your-brand-instagram).

YouTube

Most people are already familiar with watching videos on YouTube, the video-sharing website. However, it may not have occurred to them to use it for business purposes. Not only can you search for product videos, but you can also use it to vet overseas suppliers. You can see whether suppliers have uploaded videos of their warehouses, which helps you to determine whether a company is legitimate. Shreyans Parekh confirms that YouTube is especially helpful if you are thinking about sourcing from (or selling to) other countries:

> Our YouTube channel has over 25,000 subscribers and over 3 million views. We were one of the first in the industry to adopt video, and it has been especially successful for us in the international market. We'll get YouTube subscribers from South America and Brazil who want to see how certain products are used. Clients have told me that the ability to see a video is an absolute necessity for truly grasping what the product is like in real life. We have nearly 200 videos on our YouTube channel, and I am currently in the process of finding ways to further leverage this video content to trade clients. Forums and sites such as TopTenWholesale.com can be good for this purpose.

TIP

TopTenWholesale.com TV also can help you to vet suppliers. It's a video hub dedicated to the wholesale industry, with videos featuring products, companies, global trade, trade shows, and more. You can see suppliers' videos and ensure that they are up to date with the latest trends and production methods. I'll also discuss more features of TopTenWholesale.com/TV in Chapter four.

Each of the social media tools that I have mentioned can be used for similar purposes. However, they cater to slightly different audiences and have unique functions. I highly recommend trying all of them out and seeing which ones work best for your sourcing and selling purposes.

Mobile Applications

Mobile applications are another way to stay up to date on industry news. Zite, for example, is a mobile phone application for iPhones, iPads, and Android phones. It searches millions of stories on the web to find articles that best match your interests. When it encounters the articles that are most appropriate for you, it delivers them to your mobile phone and creates a personalized newspaper catered to your interests. This makes searching for industry-related topics and trends easy. You can set up as many keyword searches as you'd like. I suggest starting with "sourcing," "import," "export," "manufacturing," and other terms relevant to industry jargon and areas of interest affecting global and domestic trade. This helps you to become quickly immersed in the information and lingo that are important to your industry. Although I highly recommend that you invest in a smart phone or a tablet, you also can achieve a similar service through the use of Google Alerts. Just create a Google e-mail account (which is free), and this service will bring you news related to the keywords that you select.

Newsrooms and Blogs

Of course, you will also want to search for news on your own when you have the time. Table 2-1 lists some specific online newsrooms and blogs that feature professional and relevant content. Each website is related to a different aspect of the sourcing business and will help you to become familiar with jargon and events from various areas of the sourcing industry.

TABLE 2-1   Sourcing News Resources

SourcingJournalOnline.com	A global news resource with information for business executives who want to know about supply-chain-related topics within the soft goods and textile industry.
Blog.trade.gov	Tradeology is the official blog of the International Trade Administration, which discusses international trade laws and agreements.
Manufacturing.net	Shares manufacturing industry–related news, opinions, and trends related to the global manufacturing community.
Nam.org	A newsroom hosted by the U.S. National Association of Manufacturers shares manufacturing industry–related news.
Retailminded.com	Has a wealth of resources throughout various sections of the site, and the blog covers retail industry news and practical advice.
TopTenWholesale.com/news	Covers wholesale industry news related to topics including company profiles, the wholesale industry, product news, trade shows, marketing, business, and Asia.
Tsnn.com	Is the world's leading online resource for the trade-show, exhibition, and event industry.

Business Networking Mixers, Seminars, and Events

Attending business networking mixers, seminars, and events is another important way to stay current with industry happenings and find opportunities related to business and entrepreneurship. You can attend them at trade shows (which I will discuss in depth in Chapter 5), or you can find these types of events year round by calling your local government's small-business administration office or your local Chamber of Commerce. Megy Karydes, board member of the Fair Trade Federation and founder of www.World-Shoppe.com, agrees that asking about seminars and events happening near you is helpful: "You should check with local associations such as the Chamber of Commerce because these people can lead you to amazing contacts."

• • •

Meetup.com is a great website that can help you to find events in your industry. There are meet-ups for business-networking events where you can connect with other professionals. Dominica Alicia, online marketing and client attraction strategies specialist, shares her experience with meetup.com:

> Meetup.com is really great; however, you need to choose carefully. Always ensure that the group has a decent number of members, they regularly organize their meet-ups, the meetings are consistent, a good number of members attend, they have positive testimonials, and people like the group. You want to join a lively and buzzing group, as networking takes time, and as you know, nobody can give time back to you. Ask yourself how the group can help your business and be clear about what you want to receive from attending this meet-up. Personally, I really like meet-ups and regularly attend two to three related to my industry weekly. I am really happy with the results.

Business-to-business (B2B) trade platforms also host industry-related networking events that you may want to attend. For example, on August

24, 2012, TopTenWholesale.com hosted a post–SOURCING at MAGIC event for the China Chamber of Commerce for Import and Export of Textiles (CCCT). Over 40 apparel and textile manufacturers from China came to Los Angeles after the trade show in Las Vegas. They went on a tour of the Fashion Institute of Design and Merchandising (FIDM), Cal Mart, and downtown Los Angeles. I also brought them to a supplier-matching event where over 75 importers, brands, and entrepreneurs got to meet with these exporters. The only way to find out about this event would have been by being a community member of TopTenWholesale.com or Manufacturer.com, word of mouth, or following events closely on Eventbrite.com. However, to find out about these types of happenings, I recommend subscribing to B2B platforms' newsletters; it's the easiest way to see what events they're hosting.

TIP

To stay organized and avoid inundating your inbox with alerts, you can create a folder in your e-mail for newsletters and meeting updates. This gives you the ability to easily reference the news and events that are relevant to you and your business.

There's a wealth of information and loads of communities that can assist and inspire your business. It's just a matter of starting the investigation process and deciding what's most helpful to you. The more immersed you are in your industry and its happenings, the better chance you will have of achieving success.

Scott Steele, president and publisher of the trade publication *Canadian Merchandiser*, shares the importance of accessing as much information as possible:

The best advice I can give to anyone looking to get in to this industry is that information is crucial. Any source of reliable information, whether it pertains to suppliers, product trends, or industry news, is a valuable tool. It can come from many different sources, including trade magazines, websites, trade shows, speaking with suppliers, or picking the brains of people who are already doing what you want to do. Gather as much information as you can before entering into this; it is extremely valuable, and you can never get enough.

RESOURCES FOR SMALL BUSINESS AND ENTREPRENEURS IN LOS ANGELES

Stephen Cheung, managing director of the international trade and clean tech sector in the Office of Economic and Business Policy for the Los Angeles Mayor Antonio R. Villaraigosa, shares some of the resources available to assist small businesses in Los Angeles:

We absolutely want to facilitate the growth of small business in Los Angeles. We are the home of well over 300,000 small businesses, and entrepreneurs are the backbone of our economy. To assist small businesses, local, state, and federal governments have many incentives that are available to help entrepreneurs in LA. Our website is a great place to start looking at the many incentives available: www.losangelesworks.org/resources/incentive-by-zone.cfm.

Besides incentives, there are partnership opportunities with the Small Business Administration and the Los Angeles Economic Development Corporation that could help guide entrepreneurs through the complex process of starting a new business: http://laworks4.biz/Home.aspx.

Furthermore, Los Angeles has a number of different programs dedicated to supporting trade opportunities. For example, the Port of Los Angeles has the Trade Connect Program. Trade Connect is an introductory workshop on the basics involved in exporting, including costs, risks, and steps. In cooperation with other agencies and professionals, a summary of help and services available is presented, including

- The basics of the commercial transaction
- How to find overseas markets

- Trade financing
- Documentation

In addition to the provision of expert services, practical techniques of risk mitigation are presented at the workshop. This program connects businesses with the essential resources provided by the following governmental entities:

1. Federal:
   - U.S. Department of Commerce
   - U.S. Export Import Bank
   - U.S. Small Business Administration (Export Assistance Center)
   - U.S. Southern California Regional District Export Council
2. State:
   - California International Trade Development Centers (California Community Colleges)
3. City:
   - Port of Los Angeles (including overseas offices)
   - Los Angeles World Airport (LAWA)
   - Minority Business Opportunity Center (MBOC)

For more info about this program, go to www.portoflosangeles.org/business/trade.asp.

One final resource worth mentioning is the Los Angeles Regional Export Council. The council aims to streamline export services in the LA region and help companies find the services they need to grow their business and create new jobs. You can find out more information about this initiative at http://mayor.lacity.org/PressRoom/LACITYP_020011.

Although many of you may not work in Los Angeles, the preceding is a good example of the type of assistance and planning that local, state, and federal governments provide to small businesses. Contact your local mayor's office to see what kinds of opportunities are available in your state.

The Importance of Opening Your View to All Sourcing Resources

Now that you understand how using and engaging with a multitude of social media, news sources, business networking events, and government resources helps you to stay on the vanguard of product and industry news, you are ready to see how a similar approach applies to the use of product-sourcing resources.

Product sourcing is very dynamic. There are always new suppliers joining the market, and the products you sell are constantly evolving. Keeping a close watch on market developments ensures that your business and products don't go out of date. It also helps you to expand and grow your business when necessary.

• • •

Shreyans Parekh, cofounder of Koyal Wholesale, explains how he knew that it was time to look for new products and expand his business:

> When we first started, we focused on glassware. Then, step-by-step, we have grown to source products from all over the world and add in new product categories. There was a need in the market for more than glassware, so we had to do more. Glassware is the crucial element of the centerpiece for floral arrangements, so we began to look for additions to glassware for the centerpiece table. We started from the center point and expanded outward with floral lighting, ostrich piecing, and diamond decor. The demand kept growing and has never stopped, bringing us to where we are today.

To meet your customers' needs, you will eventually want to find new products. The best way to do this is by using multiple sourcing resources. If you repeatedly stick with the same methods, your business can become stagnate. Using only one approach doesn't allow you to see the whole scope of products in the market. Participating in various sourcing methods gives you access to all available information in your industry and the opportunity to meet the full gamut of suppliers available.

Having more than one supplier to choose from is not only important for ensuring that you are getting the best products, but it also will help you to compare the quality, prices, and services that different suppliers offer. And it helps you to avoid problems if anything goes wrong with the ones you are working with. Marc Joseph, CEO and president of DollarDays International, Inc., makes clear the importance of having various sourcing methods and backup suppliers:

> It's good to have a variety of sourcing methods. You want to make sure that you have a backup vendor for every product you buy. Seventy-one percent of companies go out of business by their seventh year. If a key vendor goes under, it's good to have another option to replace them. You can't put all your eggs in one basket and let them affect your success.

Creating a database provides you with an easily accessible backup list of suppliers. It allows you to be prepared for any changes that may occur. For example, you have the ability to maintain an advantage if your supplier tries to unreasonably raise its prices. If you know that you have other options available, you will have the confidence to tell the supplier that you can get better quotes elsewhere, and you have more negotiating power. Moreover, having many suppliers accessible ensures that you don't rush into any relationships that aren't right for you. Finding the right supplier can make or break the strength of your supply chain, so I insist that you search through an abundance of resources to find the perfect trading partners.

How to Diversify Your Approach to Sourcing

To have an abundance of suppliers at your fingertips, you need to step out of the silo and use a diverse group of resources and methods for sourcing. The key areas of diversification for product sourcing can be broken down into the following methods: trade shows, online B2B trade platforms, and B2B print media/magazines. Let's look at how to diversify in each of these areas more closely.

Trade shows are an important part of expanding your chances to obtain new products and meet new suppliers. Most people starting out in the wholesale and retail business know that trade shows are important but do not know how to find the right shows to attend. I will cover how to find them in depth in Chapter 5, but for now, it's important to understand that it's smart to attend various shows that meet your needs. Attending multiple shows allows you to see which options give you the best quality, service, and supplier base. For example, if you are in the housewares industry, the International Home + Housewares Show, ASD, the New York International Gift Fair, and the National Hardware Show are popular choices. However, you will not fully understand the resources available to you by attending only one of these shows. Each of the shows has different products, seminars, and networking events. Going to all of them helps you to meet new people and form a network that will fuel your passion and enthusiasm. You never know what new suppliers or products you can find or what contacts you can meet to bring you to the next level in your business.

• • •

In addition, by trying out different trade shows, you will eventually come to realize which shows are the most essential to you. You won't have to go to all the shows every year, but knowing the pros and cons of each event provides you with familiar backup options. This helps you to quickly find new opportunities if one day the shows you attend regularly fail to meet your needs.

Furthermore, there are different types of shows, and each one has distinct benefits. Attending more than one show will allow you to experience the differences and decide which is right for you. Lisa Gleeson, founder and owner of Lisa's Gift Wrappers, explains why she attends both regional and national shows:

When you are first starting out it's important to go to lots of shows. It's a great way to do market research and see what other companies are doing. Also, it's a good idea to attend both regional and national shows. They are good for different purposes.

When I go to a regional show, it's usually to look at what's happening in my corner of the world. As it's a smaller show, it's easier to see everything, and I don't get lost. Sometimes national shows have an extremely vast number of products, so it's easier to get lost. Also, regional shows give me the chance to go back to booths and talk more in depth with artists. I like to find out what influences their designs and businesses. Additionally, going to a regional show often means that I'll get to see my own rep (which doesn't always happen at national shows due to traveling expenses). This is good because they have insight into what's selling in my region.

The downside to a regional show, though, is that emerging artists from elsewhere often only attend national shows. To find new artists outside my region, I attend the National Stationery Show (NSS) in New York City. This show draws many emerging and well-established artists and gives me tons of ideas about color trends, new products, and a chance to speak with vendors and manufacturers.

I also advise that you try out more than one B2B trade platform. Some people may limit themselves to one platform and think that it's providing them with a look at all the suppliers out there, but this isn't always the case. Different platforms feature different types of suppliers. Some platforms focus only on international or domestic suppliers, whereas others focus on both types. Business-to-business platforms also vary by product category; some are very specific, focusing on only one industry, whereas others are broad-based, focusing on many categories. In Chapter 3 I will explain how to know which type of platform is correct for you. However, without trying out various options, you won't get a full view of all the suppliers available. And worse yet, you won't have the ability to pit suppliers against each other when asking for product quotes.

It's good to search all relevant platforms available to you because suppliers often choose to advertise more heavily on one platform than another. By looking at various platforms, you ensure the greatest amount of supplier options and are acting as a product-sourcing specialist. Shreyans Parekh shared the array of platforms that he uses: "TopTenWhole sale.com, Alibaba.com, GlobalSourcing.com, and MadeInChina.com are all valuable sites that we go to for ideas, supplier references, and new product inspiration."

Using Business-to-Business Trade Magazines

You should also give yourself more than one option when looking at B2B trade magazines. You may have heard of the big names, such as the Merchandiser Group magazines by Sumner Communications, Inc., but there are others, such as *Retailers Forum Magazine* by Forum Publishing Co., the Hong Kong Trade Development Council (HKTDC) product magazines, and many more. In fact, there are thousands of trade magazines for product sourcing. And just as I explained with B2B trade platforms, suppliers will not have the ability to advertise in all the magazines out there. Looking at various magazines gives you the greatest possibility of seeing the full gamut of suppliers.

Scott Steele, publisher and CEO of *Canadian Merchandiser* magazine, agrees that it's important to look at various magazines:

Each B2B publication targets different types of buyers and industries. There are a large number of B2B trade publications that deal with the general merchandise industry and hit a lot of different types of buyers. Sumner Communications, Inc., where I started my career, had magazines that targeted all kinds of businesses. Some would target new merchandise, swap meet, and flea market vendors, while other publications would target the permanent retail storeowners or the e-tailor (retailers who do business primarily online). The magazines have various target audiences, but a lot of these audiences have the same buying needs and patterns. You may need to look in several publi-

> **TIP**
>
> In order to keep track of the platforms you come across, I suggest that you make a folder on your Internet search bar browser called "Sourcing Platforms," where you can bookmark the websites you find. Here you can also add a few notes about the specifics of each platform that help you to remember the types of opportunities and suppliers available on each one. This allows you to easily access the specific platform that coincides with the type of product you're looking for. It also helps you to ensure that you don't miss any opportunities when requesting quotations from suppliers.

cations to get full exposure to all the information that's useful for you.

Looking at various magazines also helps you to discover new information. Megy Karydes, board member of the Fair Trade Federation and founder of www.World-Shoppe.com, explains how she uses a variety of trade magazines, including those outside her industry, to help her spot trends:

> I recommend looking at a variety of trade magazines, even those outside of your industry. I source a lot of jewelry and fashion is what drives both industries in terms of trends. I look at fashion-related trade magazines, as well as jewelry magazines, to see which jewelry items will become popular. I also read a magazine called *American Salon* geared toward the hair industry. A lot of salons carry jewelry, so it's another way to see new styles, products, and trends.

Jeremy Shepherd, founder and CEO of Pearl Paradise, also explains how different trade magazines cater to different learning opportunities:

I read *Jewelry News Asia* because it has auction reports. The auction reports tell me whether pearl prices are rising or falling and enable me to be in a better position to negotiate. I also read *Website Magazine* in order to stay abreast of new technologies and opportunities that may arise in our industry.

Another important reason to look at a variety of B2B media publications is for the variation in editorial content. This can be very helpful for sourcing because the editorial section of each magazine has new products, product reviews, industry trends, and company profiles. Scott Steele explains a little about the editorial content in *Canadian Merchandiser* magazine and how to use it:

> We do editorial coverage on new products and new product trends. If you're looking for a new product, you can use the info from the editorial content to look for advertisers that have that product. Then you can go to their website and see the variety of products that the supplier has.

• • •

In addition, Don Davis, editor-in-chief of *Internet Retailer* magazine, explains the power of the staff behind the editorial content: "We have a team of 16 full-time journalists and researchers producing the information that goes into the magazine, our web news stories, and our research guides." With this kind of assistance, you are sure to find useful information. And reading a variety of magazines allows you to get advice and perspectives from an even larger team of journalists. The more publications you read, the more connected you will be to the industry.

Why You Should Combine Various Sourcing Methods

Not only is it necessary to consult many resources within one sourcing approach, but it is also important to combine various sourcing methods. You can start by finding suppliers in a B2B magazine, then search for

TIP

Another way to receive editorial content is by checking out TopTen Wholesale.com. It's one of the only B2B platforms that has a newsroom. Similar to B2B trade magazines, you can find great articles and content from credible industry experts. However, the added plus about newsrooms is that the content is updated daily. I also suggest that you sign up for the biweekly newsletter and subscribe to daily news alerts, which provide you with relevant sourcing-related content.

them on a B2B trade platform, and later meet them at a trade show. Or the process could happen in reverse: You can start by meeting suppliers at a trade show and later vet them through the use of platforms and/or print media.

Combining different approaches allows you to get the most out of each and leads you to find the most appropriate suppliers for your business. Yosef Martin, president of Merchandize Liquidators, LLC, agrees: "All sourcing methods are important; you just have to know how to use them." For example, Jena Hazlerigs, owner and manager of Total Pro Roofing, gives her opinion about the most beneficial uses of trade shows:

Trade shows can be a great source of information for attendees. If you're looking to learn more about your industry and the competition, this is a great way to do it. A lot of information can be discovered online, but extra details are better learned in person through spoken conversations. However, I don't see trade shows as a viable way to secure trade partners, just for knowledge.

Scott Steele explains why he recommends combining the use of trade shows and trade magazines: "Their goals are one and the same regardless of the fact that their means to achieving those goals are a little different.

Trade shows and trade magazines help each other." Trade publications can help you to find trade shows. Megy Karydes confirms, explaining that she likes to read trade magazines because "they provide information about what, when, and where trade shows related to [her] industry are happening." Scott Steele also affirms that his magazine helps readers to find trade shows: "Trade shows advertise in our magazine, and we have trade-show calendars, which give readers a full year's view of what trade shows are coming up."

While attending shows, you also should look for their media partners' magazines. They usually have trade-publication bins with tons of different magazines for you to discover. The SOURCING at MAGIC, for example, has a large variety of trade magazines. Each magazine has a separate sales team behind it looking for new suppliers in different niches. Looking at various publications, even under the same media house, will let you see the scope of suppliers available in the market.

TIP

The directories that you pick up at trade shows also can be used like trade magazines. They are like a goldmine for finding suppliers and should be saved for later reference. Both new suppliers and industry veterans can be found in these resources.

Your preference for the use and combination of different sourcing resources may vary by the type of industry you are in. Eric Shannon, cofounder of OhMyDogSupply.com, explains his approach:

For us, trade shows are the best source of new products because you can hold the products in your hands and ask questions. You can also get an idea if you will work well with the owner or representative of the product line. Trade magazines are the next best for the pet industry. I find some really great stuff advertised in trade publications that is not available in the big-box stores. Online platforms are in third place out of these three. The advantage of using them is speed and ease.

For David Stankunas, founder and owner of the soft apparel goods company Beard Head, the approach opposite of Eric's works best: "I started with B2B platforms, and they are still my favorite way of sourcing. Trade shows came later." Each resource will have different advantages based on who you are and the industry you're in. This is why it's so important to scour all the material available. I urge you to try different combinations of resources. Don't settle until you've found your perfect sourcing approach.

Additionally, if you're thinking about becoming a supplier yourself, by launching your own product line or importing goods, you need to remember to advertise in all the available sourcing resources. Yosef Martin, president of Merchandize Liquidators, LLC, confirms that a variety of resources can bring you qualified leads:

> As a supplier, you need to put yourself everywhere. That's why we advertise in industry trade publications, B2B trade platforms, and exhibit at trade shows. It brings us quality leads, gives us more credibility, and shows that we are serious.

Conclusion

I hope that you see the value in leaving no stone unturned when looking for suppliers and finding valuable business resources. Information (and knowing how to use it) is an essential part of the sourcing process. You are aware of how social media, news resources, events, and government entities help you to stay current. You know that they can spark product and business inspiration and help you to connect with relevant peers. You have learned why scouring various trade shows, B2B trade platforms, and B2B trade magazines (and using a combination of these methods) gives you the best of their attributes. Having your eye on all the resources available to you will keep you in the pulse of the industry and help your business thrive.

Looking Ahead

You may be feeling overwhelmed with the abundance of resources available to you, which is *more* than normal. In Chapter 3, I will explain the factors that help you to choose the best trade magazines, trade shows, and B2B trade platforms for you. I also will give you tips on how to select the right resources and teach you which suppliers to look for while there.

3

Sailing Your Boat in a Flooded Marketplace

Out of clutter, find simplicity. From discord, find harmony.
In the middle of difficulty lies opportunity.

—Albert Einstein (1878–1955), theoretical physicist,
philosopher, Nobel Prize winner

In Chapter 2 you learned about the importance of searching for suppliers by combining various sourcing approaches. You also learned why doing research helps you to make wiser choices for your retail or wholesale business. But how do you choose among the various sourcing resources that you come across? How do you find the resources that bring you to the people who will help to make your dream a reality? And how do you know which suppliers to choose while there?

There are a vast number of supplier options out there, and you need to know how to narrow them down. With all the places available to conduct your sourcing search and tons of suppliers for each product, it can all seem very overwhelming. But no need to worry; in this chapter I will explain how to discover and use resources that will lead you to credible suppliers with quality products. I encourage you to get excited about the opportunity to explore these many options. Having them ensures that you will see all the best suppliers out there and reap the added benefits (including business advice, product videos, and seminars) that various resources provide.

Product sourcing is less challenging when you use the right resources and know how to spot the best suppliers. When you have mastered these elements, the abundance of resources available will suddenly turn into an ideal few. You will know how to combine various sourcing approaches to help you in various aspects of your business needs. And you will have a constant influx of options for suppliers.

• • •

I can recall my first ASD Trade Show in March 2002. Ripe in the industry, I had no idea of what to expect. My only experience to date had been on the phone selling advertising space for my company's business-to-business (B2B) trade magazines and website. When I entered the Sands Convention Center for the first time, I was truly overwhelmed by the thousands of suppliers and tens of thousands of products. Trying to figure out where the best opportunities were soon became my mission. And now, my goal at TopTenWholesale.com is to help you to harvest these opportunities. This chapter will teach you how to find new trade opportunities safely and securely. Nothing is easy, but knowledge and passion (coupled with a keen sense of how to buy) will be your key to sourcing (and selling) successfully.

Finding the Right Sourcing Resources for You

Sourcing is based on relationships—it's all about who you know. You need to find the resources that are connected with good suppliers. And among those resources, you need to choose the ones that cater to your prerequisites. Finding the medium that meets your needs will lead you to the right suppliers. To evaluate whether you are using the right sourcing channel for you, there are several factors to consider. You need to evaluate your business goals, look at the added benefits the resource offers, get recommendations from industry peers, choose between free or paid services, and decide whether you want broad or granular channels.

Let's examine these elements more closely so that you can decide which media are best for you.

First, you need to know why you are attending, clicking, or visiting the resource. Is it to network, search for vendors, or brainstorm and find out what is innovative and trendy in your industry? Having clear goals will help you to determine whether you are starting your sourcing journey down the right path. Some trade magazines, trade shows, and web-based B2B platforms cater to all areas. For example, TopTenWholesale.com and Manufacturer.com have over 300 combined product categories, whereas other resources focus more specifically on one category. Navigating these waters can be treacherous if you don't have a guide. Trade shows, online platforms, magazines, and other resources are the tools you need to navigate, but let's remember that without a good teacher or mentor, it's difficult to understand how to use them. Figuring this out alone can be daunting because sourcing is people-powered. In order to find the right people, you need to form the right relationships.

Malcolm Gladwell discusses the "law of the few" in his book, *The Tipping Point*. The law of the few states: "Success of any kind . . . is heavily dependent on the involvement of people with a particular and rare set of social gifts." Your job is to find the resources that are run by people with those social gifts. You need to find the ones that have developed relationships with the best suppliers out there. The resources you choose need to be connected to the best suppliers.

Other ways to tell whether you have encountered a good resource is by examining its ability to share helpful information with you. If it can, it shows that it is involved in the industry, which may indicate that it is a credible resource. Also, you should ask yourself, How is this resource helping me to find suppliers? What benefits does this resource provide to make the sourcing process easier? Does this resource host special events? Does it provide me with supplier options that match my business goals? If you can answer these questions positively and with ease, you have found a credible resource.

It's also important to remember that each retail or wholesale business is at a different stage and looking for different kinds of assistance. This is why it's essential to evaluate exactly what you require for the phase you are in. Understanding the added benefits you want to receive from the sourcing resources you use will help you to determine which are best for you. Here's how Susan Dziadosz, founder of This Charming Candy, explains it:

> When I started my business, I mostly networked with other small-business owners in the handmade community. Over time I've begun to realize that to grow my business, reach more customers, and achieve more success, I needed to become more versed in the ins and outs of the manufacturing side of the food industry. I needed to network with other businesses that face the same issues I do (e.g., food labeling laws or safe food practices). I'm also looking forward to making connections with packaging specialists and equipment manufacturers.

To help you to decide which sourcing platform to choose, try to get recommendations from industry peers. Talk to other suppliers or retailers that you trust, and find out what they use. Keep in mind that for good reason the resources from which other retailers and wholesalers source is something many companies are reluctant to share. However, if you join associations, network locally, and scour the Internet, you'll get to know people, and they'll get to know you. At that point they may be more willing to share this kind of valuable information. These recommendations are the number one way to find the sourcing channels that will lead you to useful business information and contacts. Learning the reasons that credible people in your industry are pleased with the trade shows they attend, B2B platforms they use, or magazines they read gives you criteria to evaluate whether the resource will be helpful to you. For example, I spoke with Alain Stambouli, owner of the Via Trading Corporation (www.viatrading.com), who explained why he goes to ASD:

> We exhibit at the ASD Trade Show twice a year. It's the biggest show in the world for closeout goods, and our consistent presence there has helped us in multiple ways. We've been able to establish ourselves as a reputable company in the liquidation/closeout industry, expand our customer base, and expose our company

name and products to the tens of thousands of wholesale buyers who visit each year. And our trade-show exhibition is complemented by a tremendous amount of postshow and preshow marketing. We utilize online B2B platforms like TopTenWholesale. com and advertise in trade magazines like *SoloMayoreo*.

You can find out more about the suppliers who exhibit at ASD on TopTenWholesale.com/news in the Trade Show section. Discovering what magazines the major players in your industry read, which trade shows they attend, and the B2B trade platforms they use leads you to the resources that have helped them to achieve success. It also will help you to identify new-product sourcing resources.

In addition, I advocate careful and targeted Internet searches to help you to discover prospective sourcing channels and suppliers. Before you make a decision to use a resource or work with a supplier, do a search on Google, Facebook, LinkedIn, and Twitter. See what other retailers and wholesalers are saying about the resource's services. Also, if the magazine, trade show, B2B platform, or supplier doesn't have an online presence, that's often a warning sign, and you should move on to the next option. Serious sourcing resources and suppliers want to be known and will make the effort to get themselves onto your radar. Look for company reviews, posts on message boards, and forums. Also check the company out on the Better Business Bureau's and/or Dun & Bradstreet's websites.

Using Free versus Paid Resources

There's a lot of free information on the Internet, but not all sourcing resources are free. When it comes to determining whether or not to use free versus paid services, I suggest determining whether there's a reason to pay or seeing if you can find a way to access the information for free. Most of the major trade shows that I will be discussing in Chapter 5 (ASD, the Off Price Trade Show, the National Hardware Show, SOURCING at MAGIC, and the International Housewares Show) are free. And although you have to pay small subscriptions for some trade magazines, good ones such as *Canadian Merchandiser, Retail Minded,* and *Internet Retailer* magazine have a lot of free material available online. Depending on the industry you are in, you will use both free and paid services—it's up to you to decide.

One exception, though, is with B2B trade platforms. If you are a buyer looking for suppliers, you should never have to pay to use a B2B trade platform. Don't trust a site that says that it will give you a list of secret suppliers' contact information for a fee. There are so many free and credible platforms out there that this just isn't necessary. The only people who should be paying to use a B2B trade platform are the suppliers who want additional advertising services to attract the business of retailers and wholesalers. They advertise to make themselves more available to you and prove that they're a serious company. Yosef Martin, president of Merchandize Liquidators, LLC, speaks to this point:

> You find legitimate companies on TopTenWholesale.com; they have been verified and know the important places to be in the industry. It's easier to deal with these companies because they actually had to have the funds to advertise on the platform. You know that they are serious and doing well enough to promote themselves.

Sites such as TopTenWholesale make it easy to determine between free and premium-verified suppliers, which is another indication that they are a legitimate and serious company. However, I will discuss this more in depth in Chapter 4.

Choosing Broad versus Granular Channels

You also have the option of choosing broad or granular channels. Broad resources are trade shows, magazines, and B2B platforms that cater to a wider audience with many industries combined. These resources are very efficient because major-industry players normally will attend these shows in addition to industry-specific shows. This is a great choice if you have a store with more than one type of product. It allows you to get everything done and find all the information you need in one place. Examples of broad-based resources include magazines such as those available through GlobalSources.com, trade shows such as the ASD Trade Show and the National Hardware Show, and B2B trade platforms such as TopTenWholesale.com or Made-In-China.com.

Many retailers and wholesalers prefer broad-based media. Cindy Teasdale McGowan, founder of Makaboo, shares that she likes to read general trade magazines such as *Internet Retailer* because "it gives [her] great practical e-commerce advice," and Ruksana Hussain, founder of Ideas Are Us, explains that she likes broad-based trade shows because they "give her ideas for marketing, displays, new products, color combinations, and more." And Adam McFarlane, former buyer for Walmart and CEO of Innovation Supplier, explains why broad-based shows are useful for people who want to start their own brand: "ASD is not really specific, which is why I like it. I can see everything. Also, it's really good for up-and-coming brands because you have a diverse buying group come in."

These are just a few of the many reasons why you may prefer a broad-based resource. Sometimes having the added benefit of people from an industry similar but not the same as yours can provide you with new information and opportunities. It all depends on what you are trying to achieve and whom you are trying to meet.

Granular-sourcing resources are trade publications, trade shows, and B2B platforms that target specific industries and products. You can find a niche resource for almost any industry. Some examples of resources that focus solely on one industry include trade shows such as the Gem Fair in Sacramento and the World Quilt Show in New Hampshire, B2B trade platforms, trade magazines such as *JCK* and *TDmonthly*, and online forums such as www.toydirectory.com/index.asp, www.gogift-mart.com/, www.lashowroom.com/, and http://fashionsnoops.tumblr.com. These resources focus on one aspect of an industry, and if you sell a very specific category of merchandise, these could be a good choice for you.

Daniel Villalobos II, director of sales and marketing for EasyTrac-GPS, Inc., explains that he likes specific industry-related events and publications because they have the relevant contacts and information he is looking for:

> We prefer to focus on industry-related business-to-business publications and trade shows. This gives us the ability to focus our networking on potential research and development partners and keeps us abreast of the latest developments within the wireless technology marketplace. Machine-to-machine technology is an ever-changing platform, and it requires a focused discipline to ensure [that] our sales and design teams are informed of the latest developments.

Deciding whether broad or boutique events, publications, and platforms are right for you comes down to the information or contacts you're looking for and your specific business goals. However, I recommend broad-based B2B trade platforms because they can meet broad and niche needs. When you are a member of TopTenWholesale.com, you receive invitations to seminars and sourcing events that either cover many industries at once or that hone in on niche business requirements. For example, I hosted an event in August 2012 after the SOURCING at MAGIC show where 43 premier manufacturers from China came to a supplier-matching event located in Los Angeles. This was an exclusive event where buyers from the TopTenWholesale community were invited to the Watermarke Tower for access to exporters who make all types of apparel and clothing categories. At events such as this, you can meet manufacturers who cater to your specific needs.

• • •

Hopefully you feel more comfortable with the various types of resources out there and understand how to evaluate them. If you still feel a little unsure, that's understandable. I'll discuss these resources in more depth and provide advice about how to use them in upcoming chapters. However, before I do, let's learn about the different types of suppliers you'll come across when using sourcing channels.

Types of Suppliers

Once you have verified and done some background research on the supplier with whom you're considering working, you will be one step closer to submitting requests for quotations (RFQs) on desired products in that supplier's inventory. Before you do this, though, you need to be aware that there are many types of suppliers, and each has different prerequisites for buying from them. Understanding the type of supplier that's best suited to your business model will help you to source the best products (at the best prices) and in the ordering format that works for you. This is an important component to achieving the competitive edge you're looking for. The suppliers that I'll cover include manufacturers, importers, exporters, wholesalers, distributors, and suppliers that drop ship. Let's learn more about these suppliers now.

Manufacturers produce goods. They're the source of all the goods that other types of suppliers sell. Marc Joseph, CEO and president of Dollar-Days International, Inc., explains that manufacturers are "the smartest channel to buy from because you get the items directly from the source." You're able to buy the goods at the cheapest price and are assured that the person you are buying from has a lot of knowledge about the product. The manufacturer is also a good source when you want a specific brand because you can be sure that you're getting exactly what you're looking for. You don't have to worry about knockoffs.

The down side for some to working with manufacturers, though, is that they normally require large minimum-order quantities (MOQs). An MOQ is the minimum amount of items you need to buy in a single purchase from a supplier. Manufacturers have large MOQs because they're at the beginning of the supply chain and have to cover their production costs. It often doesn't make sense financially for them to produce a small amount of a product. However, I will explain another way to work with manufacturers through manufacturers' representatives and trading companies in Chapter 6. Nevertheless, manufacturers are the best resource if you want to launch your own product line and/or would like to become an exporter, an importer, or a wholesaler.

Exporters are suppliers that sell manufactured goods from their own country to buyers in other countries, and *importers* buy goods that are shipped to their country from an exporter's country. Both are in the business of buying in large volumes because they purchase directly from manufacturers. They often store goods in large warehouses and sell their merchandise to distributors or wholesalers.

Similar to exporters and importers, *distributors* often develop relationships with and buy directly from manufacturers. However, they also can buy from importers and exporters. The main difference between a distributor and an importer/exporter is that distributors normally choose to sell to a specific region or territory in their own country.

Wholesalers can buy from exporters, importers, distributors, or manufacturers depending on the volume they sell. As Charlie Choo explains in his helpful e-book, *101 Guide to Product Sourcing Selling on eBay*, wholesalers and distributors are companies that buy goods in large quantities from manufacturers to sell them in bulk to other businesses. He further explains that to buy items from a wholesaler, you purchase products in large quantities and are charged a cost per unit. You buy at below-market prices so that when you sell the items to consumers, you make a profit. The price you pay the wholesaler is discounted based on the amount you buy; the larger the order you place, the more of a discount you'll receive, which will lead to higher profit margins. The nice thing about wholesalers, though, especially if you're a small business just starting out and/or have little capital, is that their MOQs vary greatly and are always less than those of importers, exporters, and manufacturers. *They are the best supplier choice for small retailers.*

However, it's important to remember that buying the maximum amount of products possible in one purchase from a supplier is usually to your advantage. This will render the best margins and lead to the highest profitability. Of course, this method only works if you know that the product will sell well in your store, you have the funds to buy a lot upfront, and you hold enough storage space to keep the product there while you are marketing it to your customers.

I remember my first ASD trade show years ago. It was typical to see really high MOQs. But now you can go to any trade show and discover that most suppliers have much lower MOQs and/or offer drop shipping (which I will discuss in more depth soon). And TopTenWholesale.com is the most abundant B2B U.S. portal for drop shippers and eBay products. There's an entire channel dedicated to drop shippers and eBay featuring thousands of products and hundreds of suppliers. At trade shows or online through the TopTenWholesale.com platform, you can connect with drop shippers and suppliers with low MOQs.

Minimum-Order Quantities and Warehousing Capabilities

To evaluate which type of supplier you should buy from, think about your buying power, warehousing capabilities, and sales forecasts. To save time, one of the first questions that you should ask a supplier is about its MOQ. It may be specified by a monetary amount or the amount of pieces, case packs, pallets, or truckloads you are required to buy. If the supplier's required MOQ is too big and it is not willing to compromise, then you know that you can cross that supplier off your list and move on to the next one. This is why knowing how much you want to buy and asking suppliers about their MOQs from the start allow you to save time and be efficient.

Because they are related to MOQs, warehousing capabilities are also important to consider. If you're an independent retailer, you may only have space to buy what fits in your store. If this is the case, you need to find a supplier, such as a wholesaler, from whom you can buy a smaller amount of products. On the other hand, if you are buying for a store with international shipping capabilities and need to source a large quantity of products to meet your customers' demands, you'll want to find a supplier, such as an importer, with a high MOQ. And if you are going to start a wholesale company or launch your own product line, then working directly with the manufacturer is probably going to be the right choice.

For some retailers, large MOQs can be a problem, but there are ways to work around them. Cindy Teasdale McGowan, founder of Makaboo, explains that buying large orders doesn't work for her, but she has found suppliers that understand her needs:

We need to place smaller-quantity orders on a more frequent basis. I order products once a month from our wholesalers or manufacturers, and they typically have what we need in stock. That's what works best for us. It took a while to learn that some companies just can't work that way. They need your order six to nine months in advance.

Cindy's experience shows that it's important to discuss your business model with your suppliers to determine if they're the right partners for you.

Drop Shipping and Fulfillment by Amazon as Sourcing Solutions

One solution to working around MOQs and small (or nonexistent) warehouse facilities is through drop shipping. Drop shipping allows you to source products that you never physically have in your possession. Charlie Choo explains that it's an alternative method of getting goods from suppliers. Instead of buying merchandise in bulk and keeping it in your own warehouse, you are able to have goods packaged and shipped directly from your suppliers to your customers. And you don't have to buy in bulk; you pay the supplier each time an item sells.

Doba's website (a third-party drop-ship aggregator at www.doba.com) helps to clarify that drop shipping is a supply-chain method used by suppliers that ship products for their clients directly to the end consumer. Their clients are the people who run retail stores and sell the products to the public, whereas the drop-shipping supplier stores, packages, and ships the products to the end consumer.

For some buyers, this is a great method because they don't have to place bulk orders. However, it's important to keep in mind that you don't receive as much of a discount when drop shipping as when you buy from the supplier in bulk. Remember that most suppliers are in the business of selling high volume because this is how they make money. I'll give you tips and explore more about the pros and cons of working with drop shippers in Chapter 6.

If you're thinking about using Amazon as a platform to sell your products, then consider *fulfillment by Amazon* (FBA). It is another good warehousing and fulfillment option for those who don't have a lot of warehousing space. You send your products to Amazon, and it stores them in its fulfillment centers. When your customer buys the products, Amazon will pack and deliver the items for you as well as handle customer service. You also can offer your products on other Amazon platforms outside the United States. This could be a fast and easy way for you to enter the world of global trade. Online selling expert and online selling coach Skip McGrath told us that he "loves the ease of the FBA program." You can learn more about it on Amazon's website at www.amazonservices.com.

How to Appraise Suppliers' Merchandise

After you know the type of supplier you're looking for, the next factor to consider is the type of merchandise it sells. You need to know the kind of products you're looking for, what you have a knack for selling, and what's happening in the marketplace. Marc Joseph, CEO and president of DollarDays International, Inc., advises small businesses to read and research "all the time to know what is happening in the marketplace around the world." He also suggests that they subscribe to trade publications and stay on top of national news. You need to have your finger on the pulse of market trends and stay on the cutting edge of what's happening right now. One of the main pillars of good sourcing is *arbitrage*—buying low and selling high. Doing research will prepare you to spot the hottest products at the lowest prices.

• • •

There are many tools that can help you with your product research. Skip McGrath shared that he uses two different research tools, Terapeak. com for eBay and Scan Power for Amazon. They help him to see what products are selling well and at what prices they sell. "Terapeak is a third-party research tool that allows you to know what items are selling best on eBay, their sell-through rate, what they are selling for, what key words people use to search for those items, and the time and day that those items sell most." This tool is also helpful for items he sells on other platforms: "If an item is a big seller on eBay, then it usually sells well on Amazon."

However, Scan Power is the specific tool that he uses for researching the performance of products on Amazon. "It's an iPhone application that allows you to scan the bar code of a product into your phone. It then shows you what the item is selling for on Amazon." Skip also explained that this is a great tool to use when you are in a wholesaler's or distributor's warehouse or at a trade show. It can help you to make purchasing decisions and double-check suppliers' prices. In real time, you're able to see if the price you're paying for an item will generate a profit when it sells at the retail level. The application lists how many sellers there are, the competing price for the item, whether Amazon (the company) is selling the item (which can be a tricky competitor, especially if you want to sell through its site), and the item's sales rank on Amazon. Skip always looks for products with a good sales rank because it shows how many times a day an item is sold. Usually, if the item sells well on Amazon, it has a high probability of doing well in your store. When Skip can't find the exact product model he's looking for on Amazon or eBay, he searches for similar products and does the same comparison with other brands of the merchandise. This allows him to see similar products in the market and determine whether the suppliers he's thinking about working with have reasonable prices.

Classification of Goods

Knowing the different classifications of general-merchandise goods can help you to make distinctions among suppliers and narrow down the ones with whom you want to work. There are many categories of goods,

---

TIP

Skip McGrath also explains that researching suppliers' products while product sourcing is a critical stage in a retailer's process: "Since you make money when you buy, not when you sell, you need to buy the right items at the right price to have success."

including branded products, new merchandise, used merchandise, off-price goods, closeout merchandise, and liquidation items. To determine the types of goods that you want to purchase, you need to consider what fits best in your store and what sells best in your market.

Let's define these terms to help you understand the classification of merchandise that you'll encounter during your search:

- *Branded products.* These are goods manufactured under a specific product name.
- *New merchandise.* This is merchandise that is new and has not yet been sold at the retail level.
- *Used merchandise.* These are goods that have already been sold and used at the retail level.
- *Off-price goods.* These are items that are sold between 20 and 70 percent below the regular wholesale price. David Auren, an executive at Boulevard Apparel, specializes in buying off-price goods. He explains that often he buys off-price goods at a lower price than the cost of production. Some people are weary of buying off-price goods because they think that something is wrong with them. However, this is not always the case. David clarifies some of the many reasons that goods can become off-price: "Often a manufacturer will get stuck with the goods that they produce and need to get some of their money back, even by selling the goods at a loss. This can happen because of order cancellations, overproduction, and late deliveries."
- *Closeout merchandise.* This is merchandise that is sold at or below original wholesale value. This can be the result of store closures, seasonal goods, product or package changes, overpurchasing, cancellations, and more. David Auren adds that when buying closeout items you usually have to take the entire lot of stock that the supplier sells.
- *Liquidation items.* The website liquidationcloseouts.com explains that liquidated items can be referred to as "overstock closeout merchandise." They're often brand-new items that were taken off the shelf owing to overstock, surplus stock, and end-of-line stock.

Nevertheless, liquidated products also can be from companies that have gone out of business. New Venture Media's *The Liquidators Guide* from 2011 shares that liquidated items also include slow-selling items, seasonal inventory sold to recoup capital, items that cannot be restocked because of the manufacturing becoming obsolete, launching of new models, cancellations due to delays in shipments, and damaged or compromised goods.

An Insider Look at Selling Off-Price, Closeout, and
Liquidation Merchandise
David Auren, an executive from Boulevard Apparel, gave us some important tips to buying off-price and closeout merchandise. He explains that entering the business of selling this type of merchandise is very similar to selling other types of goods—you need to network, have lots of patience, and stay current with industry knowledge. When buying products, he "always looks a season ahead and think[s] about what will become trendy in the market."

However, he also adds that buying off-price or closeout merchandise does have some differences from buying regular wholesale goods. In addition to finding goods at the right prices, the way the merchandise is shipped also matters. Soft goods come in two ways: prepackaged or assorted. Soft goods are usually prepackaged when the manufacturer has received a preorder cancellation from a retailer. David prefers buying prepackaged merchandise because "it normally comes in an organized fashion with the whole gamut of sizes. Price and size charts are also included. This makes it easier for us to sell to retailers and for them to sell to their customers."

David further explains that assorted goods are usually on the opposite end of the spectrum: "They're normally the result of merchandise closeouts, where the items that were not selling are all sold together." With assorted goods, you usually receive a mixture of products, and the full gamut of sizes is not included. With this in mind, assorted goods can be harder for wholesalers to sell to retailers. Frequently retailers want to have the full array of sizes available for their customers. Even so, it all depends on the kind of retailer that you are. If you sell individual items on eBay or Amazon, having only one size or variation of a product could be an opportunity for you, especially if you sell through auctions.

Considering liquidation products also can yield a solid profit opportunity. Store returns in particular sell for just a fraction of their wholesale cost. And most of the products are fully functional. According to Genco Marketplace, America's largest wholesale source for retail return lots, the company's most successful buyers report a 25 percent net profit margin on return lots. This is after all product, freight, and overhead expenses have been applied.

• • •

The condition of products naturally affects demand and selling price. According to Tom McElroy, vice president of eCommerce for Gencomarketplace.com, returns are an overlooked profit opportunity for buyers of bulk liquidation lots. "With more people buying online, there is a growing volume of dot-com returns," says McElroy. "These returns offer buyers the best of both worlds. You can purchase at liquidation prices but get merchandise that is higher quality than returns from a national chain store. The vast majority of dot-com returns were sent back for reasons unrelated to product quality. For the most part, these are new or like-new products that come back in the original box." Genco Marketplace, which holds direct liquidation contracts with large online retailers, says that its dot-com return lots are very popular among bulk-lot buyers who sell on eBay.

Domestic versus International: Should You Source Products from Suppliers Overseas?

Another factor to consider when looking for suppliers is where they are from. There are many factors to take into consideration when deciding whether or not to source products from an overseas manufacturer. Some of these factors include the quantity you are purchasing and additional costs, time, distance, and management. Let's take a look at some of these factors now.

> **TIP**
>
> If you're interested in buying closeouts, off-price, or liquidated merchandise, try the following:
>
> - *Buying online.* TopTenWholesale.com has the largest selection of suppliers in the United States that specialize in closeouts, store returns, shelf pulls, and liquidations. Just visit TopTenWholesale.com, and click on the closeouts category from the homepage.
> - *Buying off line.* Attend the Off Price Trade Show and/or the ASD Trade Show. The Off Price Trade Show is dedicated to these types of goods, and the ASD Trade Show also has a whole section for these items.
> - *Understand the vernacular.* It's very important to understand the meaning of the vernacular in the closeout industry. Via Trading publishes a great glossary of terms with definitions for each category (www.viatrading.com/wholesale/456/Glossary-of-Terms.html), which is also available in Appendix B of this book.

Quantity You Are Purchasing and Costs

Many people believe that working with a supplier located overseas is the cheapest option. They think that the low labor and production costs will keep their overhead down. While this may be the case for many, it's not the case for everyone. I spoke with Michael Zakkour, a principal at Technomic Asia (a wholly owned subsidiary of Tompkins International), who shared some ideas to take into consideration when determining whether working with a supplier located overseas is right for you. He explained that when deciding whether to source domestically or internationally, it's important to think about what your first order is going to look like. Michael advises sourcing domestically if you're not ordering a large amount of products from the supplier.

If you have a great idea and want to test the product out, you shouldn't necessarily go offshore. What you think you're going to be saving and what you are actually going to save could be completely different numbers. China and many other overseas operations are not usually built for small batch orders; they're built for mass production.

Michael explained that in China, for example, manufacturers operate on 2 to 3 percent margins:

Let's say you order 1,000 units of a product that costs $5 to make and you spend $5,000 in total. With the 2 to 3 percent margins that the Chinese manufacturer makes, they will only earn $150. A company overseas may not want to work with someone 8,000 miles away for such small earnings. The additional communication costs alone could make the project profitless. By thinking about sourcing from the supplier's perspective, you see that many times it doesn't make sense for manufacturers to take on small-batch orders.

Michael explained that thinking about the sourcing equation from both sides is crucial for success. However, it all depends on the type of product you are sourcing. I spoke with David Stankunas, founder of Beard Head, who shared a different perspective: "Yes, some manufacturers will require very large orders, but some will not. My experience in the jewelry and soft-goods industry has been that even for an original custom design, you only need to spend about $5,000 to get a manufacturer in China to make it."

You may be able to find a manufacturer that will want to work with you, even when spending a smaller amount of money; it just depends on the supplier and product type. Also, you always have the option of working with a trading company if you can't find a manufacturer to make the quantity that you want to purchase. (I will discuss trading companies in depth in Chapter 6.)

Product Development

Product development is another factor to consider before sourcing overseas. Michael Zakkour suggests that if you're looking to manufacture products abroad, they should be fully developed before you go. He said that he has seen many people go to China with 80 percent of their product designed and developed, and they want the Chinese manufacturers to take them to the finish line. He explained why this is not the best plan: "Chinese manufacturers are not in the business of completing the engineering for you. Their only job should be making the product." He also warned that when you get them involved in product development, you've given them your intellectual property without protection. He advises having trademarks and patents done in China before you make your first order.

However, I would like to clarify that seeking patent and trademark protection in China is usually reserved for larger companies. It's not typically advisable for newbies and small businesses. It's very expensive to seek intellectual property (IP) protection overseas, and enforcing your IP protection is more than a full-time job; it requires an abundance of resources. Also, David shared that he prefers getting prototypes made in China: "Whenever I have used domestic sources for prototypes, they have always turned out terribly. In China, it's faster, and the quality and response are better."

Time and Distance

Many of the countries that are popular to source from overseas are very far away. China, for example, is approximately 7,000 miles from the United States. You need to take this into consideration because it's more difficult and time-consuming to manage long-distance relationships. Preplanning becomes more important. You have to be aware of holidays not only for your country but also for the country with which you're working to ensure that you receive merchandise on schedule. Managing your supply chain is important. It builds credibility and trust with your customers.

• • •

Dominique Castro, cofounder of Twistlets, explains why this is so important:

> We were so excited because we sold our product to a big-box retailer. The retailer placed their first order, and we thought they were just testing the product out to see how it would go. We assumed that we would have time to produce more of our product and fulfill the order if they reordered. However, this wasn't the case. The retailer loved the product so much that they immediately placed another order for several thousand pieces. And the timing could not have been worse.
>
> It was the beginning of January, when China's Spring Festival was around the corner, and anyone who sources from China knows that during this time of the year the country shuts down, and no business takes place for a month. Even after the festival is over and people are back at work, manufacturers have a pipeline built up, so there are many delays in receiving product shipments.
>
> So I was on the phone with the largest toy store in the world telling our buyer that although they loved the product, I couldn't meet their PO [purchase order] on this second order because China was on vacation. And the gasp that came from the other end of the line made me want to curl up and die because of all the time, effort, and energy that we had spent breaking into the market. We had made it, and then we couldn't deliver. The buyer did end up taking a smaller shipment of what we had on hand, but now they couldn't fully trust that we could keep up with production.

Dominique's situation is a great example of why it's important to know the ins and outs of the place you are working with and have a close connection with your factory. You need to be able to trust your collaborators to make arrangements so that merchandise arrives on time with the level of quality that you expect.

To avoid these types of issues, Michael Zakkour believes that you shouldn't place a manufacturing order overseas without having someone on the ground in the country to manage it for you. He suggests going yourself, having an employee go, or investing in a manager who lives in or travels often to that country. Trading companies, which, again, I'll explain in Chapter 6, may be a great solution for these types of issues.

Ability to Visit the Factory

Jay Cheng, CEO of J Goodin (the largest distributor of fashion rings in the United States), shared that success is a result of the people you work with. Here Jay explains why you should meet the suppliers you collaborate with in person:

> One time we had a factory plant manager who seemed like a great guy when we hired him. He was very smart, seemingly kind-hearted, and listened to what we wanted. It took us three years to find out that he was purposely allowing our front processes to fail by 50 percent. We pay by the piece, so the workers in step two would have to do twice as much as they normally would to make up for the failure on the first unit. However, the manager let this happen because the people in processes one and two would give him a kickback of their pay. They wanted the opportunity to get more money.

Jay acknowledges that there are good and bad people/suppliers everywhere. However, he feels that the chance of getting taken advantage of is greater when you're not able to visit your factory. To ensure capital safety and product quality, it's always best to send someone you trust or go to the production facilities yourself.

Michael Zakkour explained that if you do choose to invest in onsite management and quality-control costs, you should except to pay an extra $7,000. With the approximate $3,000 for a shipping container, $1,000 for insurance, $1,000 for customs and clearance fees, and other costs for tariffs, shipping trucks, and so on, it could make more sense to

> ### TIP
>
> You can always use the resources from a site such as TopTenWhole sale.com and/or Manufacturer.com to help you find verified suppliers and get recommendations about honest manufacturers who have lead to others' success. Working with verified suppliers will greatly increase your odds of finding a reputable trade partner. However, there's no way to replace the value of a personal relationship.

produce or find your product locally. "Of course," Michel clarifies, "it all depends on the product and the cost to produce that product." To help you to determine whether going overseas is right for you, Michael suggests putting together a spreadsheet that accounts for all costs, both real and opportunity.

Being Aware of U.S. Customs Laws, Trade Agreements, and Currency

Megy Karydes, board member of the Fair Trade Federation and founder at www.World-Shoppe.com, explained some additional factors to take into consideration when importing products from suppliers overseas. They include U.S. customs laws, changes in trade agreements, and fluctuations in currency.

To understand customs laws, Megy explains that it's important to work with a customs broker. A customs broker can help you to understand the rules and regulations on importing products (such as which ones are illegal to bring in), as well as premiums put on products. Customs brokers also can help you to understand the actual cost of the item with shipping and importing fees included. Megy explains why this is so important:

One time I bought sterling silver in Pakistan, and it seemed like a great deal. Originally, it only cost $5 a unit. But, after all the

customs duties and shipping charges, the product ended up cost-
ing me $15 a unit. The additional fees made the product's retail
price jump from $15 to $45. Unfortunately, I knew that customers
weren't going to pay that price for this product.

Being aware of customs and shipping fees will help you to determine
whether overseas sourcing is truly the option with the best value.

TIP

"Working with experienced vendors lessens difficulties when importing," explains Alain Stambouli, CEO of Via Trading. He suggests
"try[ing] to find vendors who already have experience exporting the
types of products you're bringing to your country. Jewelry, children's
toys, food items, and cosmetics can be regulated very differently
around the world." If the supplier has experience exporting to your
country, he or she can help you to understand any additional costs
and/or regulations that may apply when importing your products.

Trade Agreements

You also need to be aware of changes in trade agreements. Megy Karydes
had an experience in which a trade agreement dramatically affected
a product that she was buying. "The duties on a product that I had
repeatedly bought suddenly raised my costs by 11 percent on the value
of the goods." An 11 percent increase can completely change your costs,
especially on a big order, so it's important to be aware of these types of
laws and regulations. Check out news on government websites such as
www.ustr.gov/trade-agreements to stay current on trade agreements in
the United States.

Currency Changes

You also have to watch currency changes when buying from abroad. Megy Karydes shares why:

> I have never bought anything in South Africa, where the price for the second order remained the same as the first. Sometimes the fluctuation is severe, while other times it's not. One of my secrets is that I buy a country's currency at a low rate and then let it sit in the bank until I want to buy from that country again. If you have the cash, it's a smart thing to do to secure costs.

Buying a country's currency in advance helps you to avoid paying more when it fluctuates. The currency can stay in the bank, and then you are free to buy merchandise whenever you'd like. This ensures that you get the goods at the same price as when you first ordered them. This is especially useful if you don't have a lot of storage space but know that you would like to reorder a product in the future. You can calculate currency rates at www.xe.com/ucc/.

History, Development, and Maturity of the Country

Michael Zakkour also explained that when choosing the country with which you will work, it's important to understand the history, development, and maturity of the country. "You can go to India, and the production costs will be less than in China, but the infrastructure, ports, and potential lack of history in making the product may not help you to save. You are building a relationship, and it's not all about saving money on the product."

Communication Over Price

Dominique Castro, cofounder of Twistlets, shares the importance of choosing suppliers overseas based on communication and not focusing simply on price:

Once I chose a packaging company for its low price; that was a mistake. We had a nightmare of a time communicating, which delayed the finalization of package design and production. Quality and being able to communicate with ease are more important than price.

Jay Cheng also agrees that low prices should not be your focus: "Getting the best deal should never be the first thing you look for in a supplier. Look for one that provides value, service, consistency, and quality."

Price is not the most important aspect of product sourcing. When deciding whether to stay local or go overseas, you need to think about the quantity you're ordering; the cost of the product; related fees involved with shipping, tariffs, currency, and factory management; the country's infrastructure; and your ability to communicate and build a strong relationship with the supplier.

Using Business-to-Business Trade Platforms for Due Diligence

If after reviewing the fees and risks associated you feel that going overseas is right for you, Michael Zakkour recommends using a global trade platform as a due-diligence tool. You can search for suppliers, production costs, and other important information. Each place that you choose to source from, whether it's in Asia, Europe, South America, or North America, will have its strengths and weaknesses. They all have different types of infrastructure, ways of doing business, and ways of communicating. This is why it's important to speak to people who have experience working in your prospective sourcing country. Get all the facts before wiring your money.

Sourcing from Overseas with Success

I'll discuss more about how to build relationships with suppliers in upcoming chapters, but for now it's important to know that although there are more risks involved when sourcing overseas, it still provides great opportunities for success. I spoke to many entrepreneurs who manufactured goods in other countries without visiting their factories and still achieved success.

• • •

Talia Goldfarb, cofounder of Myself Belts, shared that she has a great relationship with her manufacturer, thanks to the communication tools of the twenty-first century:

> We went back and forth with samples for quite some time to get the belts perfected in terms of how we wanted them to look, feel, and function. And then we wired money for 10,000 belts for the first order, and they arrived on a boat three months later. I still find it miraculous! I feel like I have built these quality relationships with sourcing companies that I have never met in person. You feel this bond through e-mail and can cultivate a relationship through the computer, which I am truly grateful for. I would not have a successful business if it weren't for the Internet. I have three kids and can't hop on a plane to China.

Sourcing Products from Abroad through a Domestic Distributor or Wholesaler

If you want products from abroad but aren't ready to manufacture or import them yourself, it's okay—there are other ways to get them. You can always buy products from an importer or through a distributor/wholesaler that sources products from abroad. As Gregory Lok, CEO and cofounder of Deal Décor suggests, "Think big, start small, and move forward. Think about where you want to be in five years." Maybe your goal is to manufacture your own line or be an importer and work with manufacturers directly, but you can always start by working through a distributor first, learn from that distributor, and work up to sourcing directly from overseas.

Added Value of Products from Overseas

Megy Karydes urges you to consider buying international products regardless of whether you source them from overseas or domestic suppliers. She feels that buying from overseas has an added value:

> You have a richer history in your retail environment when you carry products from around the world. And a lot of times the level of intricacy and detail shows a skill set passed down over generations. It sets you apart from other retailers because oftentimes you're carrying a product that a lot of other people won't have in your marketplace. It can be a great market differentiator. Just do your research and know what you are getting into. See if there's a local association, such as the Chamber of Commerce, that can help you to get started. Sourcing from overseas can be intimidating, but if you do your due diligence, it can happen.

Questions That Help You Determine the Right Suppliers for You

Now that you understand more about suppliers, MOQs, warehousing, products, merchandise classification, and how to determine whether to source domestically or internationally, you're ready to answer the following questions:

1. What type of supplier should you be buying from (a manufacturer, an importer, an exporter, a distributor, or a wholesaler)?
2. How do you plan on reselling the goods (through a small store to the end customer, as a wholesaler to other retailers, as a brand or importer to wholesalers, online, in a brick-and-mortar store, or another option that I haven't suggested)?
3. Do you own a small store with a physical location, or are you looking to open a store on Amazon, eBay, or the web at large?
4. What quantity of products are you looking to buy (what is the maximum MOQ size that works for you)?

5. What are your storage capabilities (do you have a warehouse)?
6. Would you like to work with drop shippers or through Amazon's fulfillment services?
7. What industry are you in, and what products are you looking for?
8. What classification of goods are you looking to buy (brands, new merchandise, used merchandise, off-price goods, closeouts, or liquidated items)?
9. Where should your supplier be located (domestically or overseas)?
10. Are you willing and ready to take the time to build a quality relationship with your sourcing partner?

As you read these questions, I hope you answered yes to the last one, but take some time now to jot down notes and come up with answers to all the questions. Having clear answers will help you to determine the suppliers that you should look for and will make your journey through this process more efficient. The more you understand your capabilities and business needs, the quicker you will find the right products and sourcing partners, which, in turn, will lead to your success. However, remember that product sourcing and supplier assessment are not a race. Maintain focus on conducting proper due diligence and qualifying every person you encounter.

Conclusion

Throughout this chapter you have learned the importance of clarifying the goals of your business to help you find the perfect sourcing resources and suppliers. You know how to find the right resources for you and are familiar with the different types of suppliers you will come across during your search. You're also familiar with the types of merchandise that you can buy and how to assess whether a supplier has sellable items at competitive prices. You also understand the term MOQ and are aware of alternative methods (such as drop shipping) for getting products if a supplier's MOQs are too high. Additionally, you're aware of the importance of working with verified suppliers and conducting due diligence (especially when thinking about sourcing from overseas). Most important, though, you have learned how to think about all these in terms of your own business needs to help you to find the right suppliers. These skills will help you to sail along more strategically as you get into the specifics of B2B trade platforms, trade shows, trading companies, and more.

Looking Ahead

Chapter 4 will discuss sourcing online and B2B sourcing platforms such as TopTenWholesale.com and Manufacturer.com. You will get a true insider's look at the best options for sourcing online. You'll learn how to navigate TopTenWholesale.com and use helpful resources such as the Wholesale B2B Video Hub, the Wholesale Trade Show Guide, and newsrooms, trade chat tools, and supplier-matching services. I will also explain how to safely use these tools and vet potential trading partners right from the start.

4

Sourcing Online: TopTenWholesale. com and Manufacturer.com

We keep moving forward, opening new doors, and doing new things, because we're curious and curiosity keeps leading us down new paths.

—Walt Disney (1901–1966), film producer, director, animator, entrepreneur

In Chapter 3 you learned how to evaluate the suppliers that you come across, as well as your own business's goals, to help you choose the right suppliers to work with. Now I will share the most crucial and readily available method for finding suppliers—sourcing online. Sourcing online is the fastest and least-expensive sourcing method available for finding manufacturers and wholesalers. Eric Shannon, a cofounder of Oh My Dog Supply, confirms, "Using B2B [business-to-business] platforms is really fast. You can search by keyword and have the contact info for hundreds of different companies within minutes." However, despite the fact that sourcing online is relatively simple, you still need to know where to look to make sure that you don't waste time with misrepresented platforms and fraudulent suppliers. This is why I am going to teach you the safest way to source online and introduce you to the best platforms available.

Importance of Using Vertical Search Engines for Sourcing

Although the Internet has emerged as a powerful way to conduct your sourcing process, you need to know how to use it effectively. Some of the best suppliers are not very good at search-engine optimization (SEO) and search-engine marketing (SEM). They don't have websites that broad-based search engines such as Google, Yahoo, and Bing can find easily.

For example, when you search on Google for the keywords "wholesale cell phone covers," there are not many search results from legitimate wholesalers or manufacturers of the product (Figure 4-1). Instead, the search results from Google are littered with well-optimized retail sites and publishers that are claiming to "sell below wholesale pricing." Even the paid advertisements (also known as *Google AdWords*) to the right of the organic search results are mere retail websites. Trying to sort through these search results would take a lot of time, and without sourcing experience, you're bound to wind up visiting the websites of dozens of unfruitful resources.

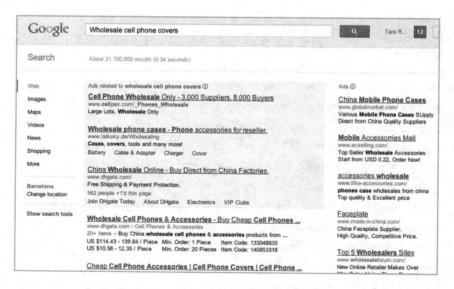

Figure 4-1 This Google search for "wholesale cell phone covers" shows how ineffective broad-based search engines can be for finding wholesale suppliers.

(Google and the Google logo are registered trademarks of Google Inc., used with permission.)

However, this is only one of the many reasons why vertical search engines (also known as *directories* or *alternative search engines*), such as business-to-business sourcing platforms, are so important. Sourcing products online with vertical search engines is also much easier because they list all the information about a specific industry or topic in one place. Furthermore, busy businesspeople in our fast-paced society want relevant information quickly. Vertical search engines make it easy to find what you are looking for and meet the demands of this fast pace. Also, the HotTopics report, "Vertical Search Delivers What Big Search Engines Miss," explains that "many professionals have learned that, as powerful as the general search is, it fails for many business-to-business uses. Failure results in productivity losses, problems finding critical content, and unmet information needs."

Although all-in-one search engines such as Google are amazing tools for many types of research, they are not the best for sourcing. They are not able to easily give you the full spectrum of sourcing partners available. They work off of algorithms and SEO, which doesn't always give you the most relevant information. And there's no verification process for whether or not these suppliers are legitimate. On the other hand, B2B trade platforms don't function by SEO and algorithms and *do* verify suppliers, which makes their results more accurate. They present you with real suppliers from relevant industries more quickly and are tailor-made for your business's success. Google is not going to assign you a trade manager to help steer communication between you and your new supplier; a qualified B2B trade platform will.

Jay Cheng, CEO of J Goodin (a wholesale fashion jewelry company), agrees that vertical search engines are more effective for sourcing:

> If you go to Google and type in the keywords "wholesale jewelry," you will get fifty thousand results and you don't know what is what or which results you can trust. But if you go on TopTen Wholesale and type in "jewelry," you are likely to find someone who is a jewelry manufacturer, especially if they are paying to be on this B2B vertical search engine. The likelihood of engaging with someone in the business of wholesale or manufacturing is

much higher on a vertical search engine. Also, as an advertiser, vertical search engines are helpful because they find your potential customer more easily than a broad-based search engine would. People who use vertical search engines are usually savvy about the business and are actually looking for wholesale suppliers.

There are many additional reasons why using vertical search engines (and in this case B2B platforms) makes your life easier. I will explain the specific benefits in more detail later, but for now, know that platforms offer you a sourcing community where like-minded people and networking opportunities are right in front of you. They make finding a supplier and inquiring about a product line, production capabilities, and minimum orders much easier.

Benefits of Online Business-to-Business Trade Platforms

Business-to-business trade platforms are vertical search engines that are designed to help you find suppliers. They are B2B communities that connect buyers and sellers in global and domestic trade. These online marketplaces provide tools that are necessary to facilitate communication between retailers/resellers and wholesalers/manufacturers. Marc Joseph, CEO and president of DollarDays International, Inc., explains: "Whether you are looking for kids' clothing or school supplies, B2B platforms are a quick way to find people. They have brought buyers and sellers together in a much more efficient manner."

Domestic versus Global and Broad versus Specific Platforms

Business-to-business trade platforms are classified by supplier reach (featuring either domestic or global suppliers) and by the industry they cater to (various or one specific market). Choice between a domestic and a global trade platform will depend partly on your minimum-order requirements and manufacturing needs. You are familiar with many of these principles from Chapter 3, but remember, if you own a small store

PASSION FOR VERTICAL SEARCH AND BUSINESS-TO-BUSINESS PLATFORMS

I am very passionate about the effectiveness of online B2B trade platforms. I know that they will bring you the best results for your business. When I began my career back in 2000, I started working for the trade magazine publisher Sumner Communications. Sumner published highly acclaimed magazines such as the Merchandiser Group magazines, *Cover Magazine*, and *Web Wholesaler Magazine*.

When I was an account executive (from 2000 to 2005), I started hearing objections from potential advertisers that print advertising was too costly and that they couldn't reach their potential buyers as easily as with online advertising. They didn't see the reason to invest in B2B print media when online media allowed them to more easily track results. They could invest the same amount of money in online marketing, and it would allow them to reach larger numbers of their target customers. Advertisers saw that they could track the return on investment (ROI) from online ads, and it helped them to make better business decisions.

It was at this time that I started to realize that not only traditional sourcing but also the ways in which buyers and sellers were connecting were changing rapidly and significantly. After fighting a battle (which seemed endless) and continually trying to sell the value of print media to clients, I accepted the market's evolution. Suppliers were making larger investments in search-engine marketing, websites, e-commerce, and SEO.

It is not to say that print B2B magazines are unimportant. I still believe that they're an important resource and that advertising in them and/or using them for sourcing is still a good idea. It's just that there are new opportunities to grow and change with the business—the emergence of B2B online trade platforms happened because the market demanded it. As Alain Stambouli, CEO of Via Trading, puts it, "B2B trading sites such as TopTenWholesale.com and Manufacturer. com have enabled us to consistently grow our global and domestic customer base, meeting the best new trading partners daily."

and need no more than 50 T-shirts, a domestic trade platform that helps
you find a supplier next door is probably right for you. And if you are
buying for a chain of grocery stores, a global trade platform that includes
resources from abroad is probably the best choice.

The type of platform that you will want to use also may depend on
how quickly you need a product. Merchandise will arrive more quickly
from domestic suppliers. If you don't have assistance in overcoming the
language and cultural barriers or in understanding the political and
economic infrastructures that come into play when working with suppliers abroad, then you may want to work with a local supplier and use
a domestic platform (even if you are a large business).

Platforms also can be either broad (focusing on many types of products and industries) or specific (focusing on only one industry). Depending on your sourcing needs, you will know which type of platform is
best for you. However, for the purposes of this book, I will be discussing
globally reaching platforms with a broad product scope. They usually
serve as a one-stop shop meeting everyone's needs.

Safety and Business-to-Business Trade Platforms

The best way to ensure your safety when sourcing online is to start with
a credible B2B platform. Some of the most reputable B2B trade platforms based in the United States include

- TopTenWholesale.com
- Manufacturer.com
- MFG.com
- Thomasnet.com

The best trade platforms based in China and Asia include

- Alibaba.com
- MadeInChina.com
- GlobalSources.com
- IndiaMART.com

I recommend these sites because they are the best known throughout the sourcing industry, and they have the most credible suppliers in their networks. However, you may come across or want to check out other B2B trade platforms during your supplier search. Let's take a closer look at how to verify that you have encountered a credible platform.

Avoiding Scams and Fake Business-to-Business Trade Platforms

When looking for B2B trade platforms, you may run into websites that advertise hidden supplier lists. They will ask you to pay a monthly fee so that you can receive "secret access" to wholesale suppliers. Beware of these sites because most of them are scams. They're trying to charge you for free information. You can get supplier lists for free on any B2B trade platform or by calling a trade show and getting a copy of the trade-show directory. As a buyer, you should never have to pay to locate suppliers. TopTenWholesale.com, Manufacturer.com, Alibaba.com, and MadeInChina.com will never make you pay for this information. These companies make money from services such as advertisements that suppliers pay them to do. They do not make money from buyers who use their platforms to source.

• • •

Yosef Martin, president of Merchandize Liquidators, LLC, explains why his company pays to be a "Supplier Pass Premium Member" and advertises on TopTenWholesale.com:

> We pay to be featured on B2B trade platforms because it brings us quality leads. I have great Internet exposure, but it's always good to put yourself in places like TopTenWholesale.com. You get leads that you wouldn't get from Google. Also, you become more legitimate by being seen in the right places where other big players are. When you have a brand, you need to pay to advertise. TopTenWholesale has been good for business, and we will keep doing business with them in the future.

Yosef makes clear why suppliers pay for you to find them and not the other way around.

In addition to not having to pay to use their services, here are some simple criteria that can help you to decide whether a B2B trade platform is worth using:

1. *There is a phone number.* You should be able to call a representative of the company and speak to someone about the suppliers on the site. You also should be able to ask any other questions that you may have about using the platform and receive assistance from a support center.
2. *You can ensure that you are engaging with safe suppliers.* The platform has a supplier verification process and explains this process to you on the website.
3. *Representatives of the trade platform attend trade shows.* They are well engaged in the business and know the suppliers on the platform.
4. *They have a high amount of website traffic.*
5. *The content is regularly updated and interactive features such as newsrooms are updated.*
6. *Many suppliers are paying to advertise on the site.* If suppliers are paying to be there, it shows that they find value in the platform.
7. *They have a newsroom, blog, video hub, answers area, and more.* The company shows a dedication to the industry and to helping buyers source safely and securely.

If a platform that you come across does these things, it's likely that it has valuable suppliers in its directory.

Importance of Working with Verified Suppliers

I highly recommend that when you use any B2B platform you focus on engaging with verified suppliers. Each site will have its own vernacular for the way it refers to suppliers that it verifies. On TopTenWholesale. com, suppliers are called "Supplier Pass Premium Members," and on

Alibaba.com they are called "Gold Suppliers." Regardless of the site you choose, focus on contacting these premium or verified suppliers. They are the most reputable, transparent, and credible suppliers available online. Suppliers on TopTenWholelsale that carry the elite status of "Supplier Pass Premium Members" have successfully passed a company profile verification (CPV).

• • •

Michael Fan, CEO of New Times, explains the importance of looking for verified suppliers when sourcing overseas:

> To find a suitable supplier in a market like China, it's always wise to choose suppliers that have been verified. Getting a recommendation or verified pass from a local platform like TopTen Wholesale.com or Manufacturer.com can help buyers find great suppliers in the shortest amount of time. The team from TopTen Wholesale knows the Chinese market and enterprises very well. They also have the advantage of knowing how to do business in both the United States and China. They can find you legitimate suppliers from anywhere with ease.

Suppliers investing in advertising are also more likely to be legitimate than not. Why spend money on an ad for many months or years if you're not? A company that can consistently pay for ads on a B2B platform isn't afraid to promote its business. Advertising space on these platforms is expensive; ads on the homepage of TopTenWholesale.com, for example, cost thousands of dollars per month. If a company can advertise consistently, it's a sign of its success and confidence in working with its customers.

Furthermore, a company that can place ads year after year demonstrates its legitimacy through the ability to remain on the site. If the company is advertising, it is usually being contacted by lots of buyers. If it scams multiple buyers who have found it through the platform, the members of the community will turn against it. The wronged buyers will tell the sourcing platform about the company and write negatively about it on forums and message boards. The supplier eventually will get exposed on these platforms if it is fraudulent.

Most companies that spend money on B2B trade platforms are confident in their businesses and what they offer. They want to meet the right trading partners and have successful relationships with them. Alain Stambouli, owner of Via Trading, explains why he uses B2B trade platforms:

> One of any company's major challenges is to get good qualified leads. TopTenWholesale.com and Manufacturer.com do a good job of qualifying their visitors and ensuring delivery of high-quality wholesale buyer leads. This, in turn, enables a high conversion ratio from lead to customer.

Yosef Martin, president of Merchandize Liquidators, LLC, also supports my advice about choosing advertising and verified suppliers when he recommends how you should vet suppliers on B2B platforms:

> If you are looking for a supplier online, you need to do a little research before you send them money. Make sure that the company is legit and that they have a website, a Facebook page, and a physical location. However, I'd say that when you are looking at TopTenWholesale.com, most suppliers are legitimate. It's safer than going to Google. The companies on B2B platforms have the money to pay for advertisements that aren't cheap but which deliver good leads. Working with advertising and verified suppliers is safer because you know that they are certified and part of the industry. You're dealing with a real company who had to put money down to be there.

Other Ways to Assess Suppliers' Legitimacy

I stand firm about choosing from among verified and advertising suppliers. However, just because a business is verified or advertising on a platform doesn't mean that you shouldn't be smart and do your own due diligence. Suppliers could lie when submitting documents and become verified suppliers without anyone knowing (until they get caught). The teams at TopTenWholesale.com and Manufacturer.com do their best to regulate the sites and audit suppliers, but nothing is bulletproof, and nobody can guarantee the business practices of other entities. Nothing can safeguard against businesses being aggressive and fraudulently representing their capabilities. Besides, this is your business and your livelihood that I am talking about. Taking extra steps of precaution never hurts. Let's discuss some specific things you can do to keep yourself safe.

First, you should make sure that the supplier is transparent. The supplier should include contact information (such as the owner's name and phone number and the company address) as well as pictures of the production facilities (especially if it is a manufacturer) on the website. You also can search the Internet to see whether the supplier is active on social media. For example, does the supplier have a Twitter handle, a Facebook business page, a LinkedIn page, or an account on other social media channels? Additionally, you should check whether the supplier is listed on other online B2B sourcing platforms and that it is findable through other sourcing means such as B2B magazines and trade shows. If you come across the company on various B2B platforms, at multiple trade shows, and in B2B magazines, there's a high chance that it is a trustworthy supplier.

The Liquidators Guide, written by Robert Cyr, provides other ways you can cross-check companies. Robert suggests looking in forums and seeing whether the supplier you are thinking about working with has any complaints raised against it. These boards often have titles such as "Good Supplier/Bad Supplier" and "Best and Worst Suppliers." Some forums that Robert suggests scouring include Wholesaleu, Wholesaleforum, RipoffReport.com, and Complaintsboard.com.

In addition, you can consult the Better Business Bureau or Dun & Bradstreet's databases to assess a supplier's legitimacy. Also, you can ask the supplier to connect you with other retailers that have worked with the supplier in the past. This is another great way to verify a supplier's services. If you can get firsthand accounts from clients who have had success with the supplier, there is no better verification process.

If you have done the preceding due diligence and believe that the supplier is worthy of your business, you are probably in good shape to go ahead and work with that supplier. However, there is one last step to being a smart buyer. When you place your first order with a supplier, avoid giving the supplier all your money up front. Use a system such as escrows to protect yourself.

Escrows are a system where a third party manages the financial aspects of your purchase order. When setting up an escrow, you give a third party all your money for the order up front. Then, once you have officially ordered the merchandise, the third-party company will send half the funds that you have deposited into the account to the supplier. When the supplier receives the money, it will start working on your order. When the order is done, the supplier will ship you the merchandise, and you will inspect it to ensure that it meets your quality standards. On finalizing the inspection, you will officially accept the merchandise (if it meets your standards) and then close the escrow account. This will release the other 50 percent of the original deposit to the supplier. This is just one example of how an escrow can be used. You can have it organized differently, but this is one smart way to use an escrow.

TIP

When working with new suppliers, escrows are a buyer's best friend. Escrow.com is a reputable third-party company that can easily help you with this process.

Doing a lot of due diligence before deciding to work with a domestic or overseas supplier is the best way to protect your business. As David Auren, executive at Boulevard Apparel, explains:

> Working overseas with someone you don't know and have never done business with can be a gamble. Tools like TopTenWholesale

.com and Manufacturer.com allow us to get a clear perspective on new suppliers. These tools let us do our due diligence to see how the supplier has done business in the past and understand how other buyers relate to them.

However, if you ever come across an illegitimate supplier on Top TenWholesale.com or Manufacturer.com, you can always report that supplier to an administrator. These sites keep data on every supplier and track every complaint that they receive. They will promptly notify the supplier of complaints. Unfortunately, a supplier cannot be removed from the site unless it is served notice from state or federal authorities. The job of the sites is to mediate the content, not disputes. The sites will, however, remove and notify suppliers anytime they are served an intellectual-property complaint. The suppliers are given 24 hours to either prove that they own the intellectual property or they will be suspended from the sites.

Finding the Best Suppliers for You on Online Business-to-Business Platforms

While on your supplier search, you will come across hundreds (if not thousands) of credible suppliers. So how do you choose the best ones? I am going to give you some simple tips that make finding over-the-web chemistry with suppliers easier and that will help you to narrow down your options.

David Stankunas, owner and founder of Bearded Apparel, Inc., explains how he uses B2B search engines for supplier searches:

I start by finding ten or twelve manufacturers that I target as potentials. Then I send out an e-mail to each of them outlining what I am looking for and wait for a response. If they don't send a response within 24 hours, I won't work with them. This is a sign of slow communication, which can lead to major problems later on down the road (especially when working with suppliers overseas). Having said that, the suppliers that do send a response within the first 24 hours move on to the next round.

Then I start the second round of cuts by reading the responses. The majority of responses that you get are cookie cutter; it will seem like many of them may not have actually read what you wrote. If the supplier doesn't address specifics from my e-mail, they are immediately out. After weeding the general replies out, I am left with two or three people who actually took the time to address my concerns in a quick manner.

Out of those two or three, there is only one who not only addressed my concerns but also asked me a lot of questions, such as, "What is the gauge on the type of yarn that you would like to use?" I go with the manufacturer that brought me their expertise and recommendations.

David also explains that you shouldn't get frustrated if you don't find the supplier you want to work with the first time around: "You can afford to be very selective because you have so many options on B2B platforms. Pick another twelve or twenty-four if you haven't found the perfect supplier for you in the first selection."

• • •

I also spoke with Mike Bellamy, owner of PassageMaker Sourcing Solutions, who gave me his company's systematic approach to narrowing down suppliers (which is also outlined on his website, www.psschina.com/):

The following is a behind-the-scenes look at how PassageMaker assists its clients in finding vendors from China. The system outlined below is based on the company's ten years of experience in China and thousands of sourcing programs.

A professional sourcing feasibility study/supplier identification research should have a clear methodology for defining and measuring the desired attributes of the ideal supplier.

Step 1: *Defining.* The right supplier is unique to each buyer, as the relative weight placed on price, quality, lead time, and other attributes differs from project to project. Below is an attribute survey template used to transfer this information from buyer to research team.

Common Key Attributes	Ranking (1 to 10)	Explanation:
Price		
Quality		
Security		Protection of IP/Non-compete
Location		Near a specific port, for example
Capacity		
Service Attitude		
Other Desired Attributes		*Such as experience with a certain technology or material, or UL certified, or possess in-house tool and die shop*

Step 2: *Measuring.* At PassageMaker, a typical supplier identification research project takes thirty to forty-five working days, assuming that multiple components and production methods need to be explored at a national level. The process is as follows:

1. Initial research. We generate a list of 50 to 100 potential suppliers using these Insider Tips:

   - Assume the vendor is a middleman until proven otherwise, not the other way around.
   - Avoid factories that refuse to list the name or location of the production facility. If they only show a Hong Kong, Taiwan, or other non-People's Republic of China

(PRC) address, they probably don't own the PRC factory and are a middleman of some sort.

- Focus on the factories that can clearly show production
  experience with your particular product or production
  method. Look for clear information about operation
  size, equipment, and staffing.

2. Review the 50 to 100 candidates' websites and brochures
against the client's desired attribute list, and narrow the
field down to fifteen or twenty candidates. At this point,
"first contact" is initiated in the following ways:

- Send an e-mail or make a phone call to ask for initial
  product-specific information (price, minimum order
  size, lead time).
- Are samples available? If they don't have samples readily available, they probably don't deal with your product on a regular basis.
- Granted the sales team will be the most polished in
  terms of English skills, but how is their understanding
  of your basic requests? If you ask for information on a
  red umbrella and get sent a sample of a blue shoe, you
  are going to have problems with communication down
  the road!
- Confirm the actual production location, and ask for
  factory ownership papers. Be explicit that the production location may be audited and that this location
  cannot be changed without approval of the buyer.

3. The preceding research should narrow the field down
to about five highly qualified candidates. At this stage,
PassageMaker Quality Control engineers and Sourcing
Managers (joined by the client when possible) visit the
factories in person to review quality systems, confirm
production methods, negotiate pricing, and look for any
red flags. In other words, visit the production facility to
confirm that the information given during the initial

research was accurate and truthful. This is an essential yet often overlooked step.

You can follow David and/or Mike's methods exactly, or you can use their advice to help you to develop your own vetting system. You know what will work best for you. I am confident, though, that by using some of their tips, you will find credible suppliers.

An In-depth User Exploration of TopTenWholesale.com

Now that you are nearly a pro on how and why to source online, you're ready to learn how to access all the benefits that TopTenWholesale.com has to offer you. I will give you a guided tour, and you'll be an expert at navigating the site in no time—not that navigating is difficult. Chase Vance, head of the student body at the Fashion Institute of Design and Merchandising (FIDM), Los Angeles, explains how intuitive the site truly is:

> As a student, I have been exposed to numerous websites and companies that connect businesses to suppliers. One of the many benefits that TopTenWholesale.com offers is its intuitive layout. Accessing information and finding suppliers on the site are easy. While working in the apparel business, finding the right vendor or factory to get the job done in a timely manner is key. You want to source quality products and receive the final product within the anticipated time frame. TopTenWholesale.com is an invaluable resource to do just that. It's great for anyone looking to get their business off the ground, as well as for businesses already thriving. It allows you to sustain and diversify your product mix and continuously satisfy and adapt to the needs of your customers.

Why Choose TopTenWholesale.com?

Before we get started, let's talk a little about what makes TopTenWholesale.com so unique. TopTenWholesale.com is a property of JP Communications, Inc., which also runs Manufacturer.com. Operating under the mantra, "Find it. Source it. Profit!" the company's search engines and directory network offer you the ability to interact with hundreds of thousands of manufacturers and wholesalers a month.

Although Manufacturer.com also can be beneficial to your business, I am going to focus on TopTenWholesale.com. It's a vertical search engine that connects buyers of general-merchandise wholesale products to manufacturers, importers, distributors, auctioneers, independent retailers, flea marketers, drop shippers, and resellers of new and closeout merchandise. It offers you the ability to source from over 20,000 domestic suppliers and 15,000 international suppliers and from 100 product categories with over 1 million products.

• • •

TopTenWholesale.com has helped many retailers and wholesalers source products for their businesses. Here is one of the many success stories from Cristy Gonzales, co-owner of CuteCDay Boutique:

I absolutely love clothing and fashion. For years I had dreamt of owning my own boutique. Finally, the stars aligned and I took the leap of faith to open CuteCDay Boutique. Finding cute, on-trend merchandise (that moves quickly) was a huge priority. It wasn't easy searching online to find wholesalers that carried what I was looking for at the price point I needed. After lots of time and research into apparel wholesalers, I narrowed down the choices to a few and placed my first orders. Luckily, I loved the merchandise and ended up choosing quality suppliers. Having a little more faith in my decision making, I started searching for new wholesalers online, which is when I stumbled upon TopTenWholesale. com. Wow! When I found TopTenWholesale.com, I saw that not only did all the wholesalers I had purchased from previously advertise on the website, but also there were so many more to choose from! It's a one-stop shop for finding quality wholesalers whose merchandise you can trust and feel confident purchasing. I now have access to hundreds of great apparel and accessories suppliers that keep my boutique stocked with cute, quick-selling, and trendy items. My customers stay well dressed and coming back for more. Thank you TopTenWholesale.com!

How to Search from the Homepage

Now you are ready for me to take you on a tour of the site. Please keep in mind that as I write this, TopTenWholesale.com is in the middle of redesigning its homepage. The screen you see while logging in may be different from the one shown here. However, the same information will be featured, and the redesign will be just as easy to use.

Figure 4-2 TopTenWholesale.com's homepage.

Let's start with the TopTenWholesale.com "arrow and target" logo in the upper-left corner of the page, which is shown in Figure 4-2. This is a quick link back to the homepage from any other page on the site. Just to the right of this logo, there are three tabs that run along the center of the page. These tabs allow you to simplify your search through TopTenWholesale's database by clicking on the one that identifies what you are searching for—Suppliers, Products, or Buyers. You will see that the default search is set up for Suppliers. To search for suppliers, you simply enter keywords that explain the type of supplier you are interested in purchasing from. If you use the advanced-search options, you can narrow down your results to only Supplier Pass and/or Premium members. Or you can search for suppliers by location. And, of course, you're welcome to leave these spaces blank and do an open search as well. Within moments, you will have a list of hundreds of suppliers that you can contact. It's that easy! When you click on the other two tabs, you'll see that the search box remains the same but allows you to select and search by specific categories. I am going to walk you through a more detailed sample product search now.

Product-Search Walk-Through
Let's search for Supplier Pass and Premium Member suppliers by using the keyword "T-shirt" in the product search box. If you do this search on your computer at home, you'll see that narrowing the search to verified and credible suppliers generates over 45 results—and generates over 199 results if you keep the search open to all available suppliers. In each of the listings of results (as shown in Figure 4-3), you are able to see whether the supplier is verified and where in the world the supplier is from, and you can contact the supplier or go directly to the trade chat (which I will discuss in more depth at the end of this chapter). For now, stay with me and learn about other ways to search.

Search by Category
If you prefer to search by browsing the items listed on the site, you can search by category. Just below the search bar (and some ads), as shown in Figure 4-4, you'll see the Top Wholesale Searches and Categories

Figure 4-3 This search result for the keyword "T-shirt" shows you how easy it is to find products and contact suppliers on TopTenWholesale.com.

sections. The Top Searches area shows you the items that are the hottest sellers on TopTenWholesale.com, as well as the categories that your colleagues and competitors are searching for most often. The top 10 most frequently searched categories on the site are Apparel, Handbags, Closeouts, Shoes, Jewelry, Computer Hardware & Software, Consumer Electronics, eBay Products, Fashion Accessories, and Dollar Store Items. However, this changes daily, so check out your screen now and see what they are today.

You also can browse any of the 50 categories available to you. As shown in Figure 4-4, when you scroll over any of the categories, you see a large array of subcategories. These subcategories help you to get an idea of what's on the site and can give you new-product ideas. This feature makes sourcing as simple as walking down the aisles of your local grocery store!

Figure 4-4   Search among the 50 categories available to you on TopTenWholesale. com to get great new product ideas.

Helpful Links at the Bottom of the Homepage

Don't overlook the bottom of the homepage. This part of the site offers you interesting information, including details about TopTenWholesale.

com and JP Communications, Inc., as well as access to the Community, Network, and Partners. I won't walk you through these items, so be sure to play around with them when you get a chance. However, I will touch on some of the features in the Community section soon when I talk about the hyperlinks at the top of the homepage.

Feedback and Support

Another helpful link that you'll find on the homepage is the feedback and support box to the middle right-hand corner of the page with a "megaphone" logo. This box is found to the middle or lower right-hand corner of the screen on almost every page of the site. This box is like your right-hand man (yes, I am aware that this is a cheesy joke). Nevertheless, I am not joking when I say that this is your trusty companion. If you ever have an issue with the site, this is where you can e-mail for support and/or give feedback to the team; team members are all ears because they want to make the buying experience incredible for you. Just simply type in the title of the message, explain what you need help with (you also can attach photos if you like), and plug in your e-mail address. Once you click the "Send Message" button, a member of the team will soon be at your service.

In the feedback and support box to the left of the screen you'll find two additional sections called Knowledge Base and Feedback. Knowledge Base lists previously submitted questions that you can browse. If someone has already asked your question (or something similar), you'll find the answer instantaneously. Also, the saved Feedback section allows you to see opinions about the site from other members of the community.

Getting Registered

You have access to many tools on TopTenWholesale.com without ever registering. However, you'll receive access to many more useful tools and can contact suppliers more easily (which I will explain in detail soon) if you do register. So let's get you registered! It's free, quick, and easy. Go back to the top of the page and just to the right of where it says "Welcome Guest," and click on the "Join Free" hyperlink. Figure 4-5 shows the simple form that you can complete faster than I can complete this sentence. You just need to fill in your country, state, trading-partner status (i.e., buyer, seller, or both), name, and contact information and create a user name and password. To consult any privacy issues that you may have, click on the "Privacy" hyperlink at the bottom of the homepage to learn how secure your information is with TopTenWholesale.com. After you type in the security figures that appear on your screen, click on the "Create My Account" button.

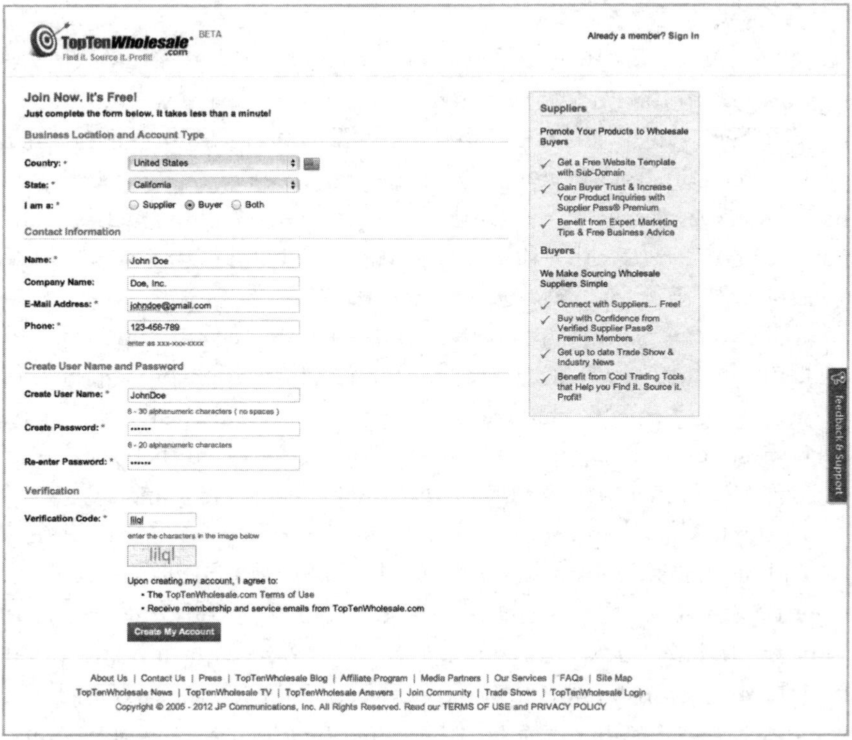

Figure 4-5 Registering on TopTenWholesale.com allows you to contact suppliers more easily.

Congratulations, you've successfully completed the first step to setting up your business on TopTenWholesale.com. Now you'll have access to tons of fun tools that you can start using immediately. However, before you get started, I suggest that you begin by filling out your company profile so that other businesses will see your professionalism and can learn more about you.

Company Profile

Adding details such as your company's logo, description, and website will help you to gain credibility among suppliers. Remember, suppliers want to work with legitimate companies, too. Filling out detailed profile information will help you to get your company's name out among your industry peers and show people that you operate a serious business. Figure 4-6 shows Via Trading's company profile. This supplier's profile is a great example of what you should be aiming to create for yourself and the type of profile you should be looking for from suppliers.

Figure 4-6 Via Trading's profile is effective because of its visual nature. Suppliers worth working with will have a complete company profile filled with photos and videos.

The more visual your profile is, the better it will be received. Using photos and videos helps to make your company more transparent (i.e., easy to understand/get to know) and accessible to others. It also shows others your business goals, which helps suppliers to determine whether they have products that will lead to your company's success. And remember, the suppliers with whom you are looking to work should have transparent visual profiles as well. Transparency demonstrates the suppliers' credibility and honesty.

Once you have completed your profile, you may be tempted to fill out the Product Requests tab. Although this is a great tool, which allows you to fill out request-for-quotation (RFQ) forms, please stay with me. I will explain more about how to do that soon.

Top-of-the-Page Hyperlinks: News, Trade Shows, Videos, Answers

Now let's take a look at the hyperlinks that run across the top of the right-hand side of the homepage. These hyperlinks consist of Sell, Buy, News, Trade Shows, Videos, Blogs, and Answers. I am not going to go through the details of each of these tabs, but I will point out the benefits of some of the most important ones.

News
Clicking on the "News" hyperlink takes you to TopTenWholesale's newsroom (Figure 4-7). This is a great resource for finding industry-related news. It's a quick and effortless way to stay on top of what's happening in the industry. I have a full-time staff that searches for relevant and trending topics in the global sourcing business. Whether you are looking for new marketing tactics, innovative products, or selling tips, you can find them all right here. I also suggest that you check out the "Recent Articles" section, which enables you to see the latest news or browse by topic.

Trade Shows
I will discuss trade shows and more about how to find them in Chapter 5. For now, it's good to know that you can quickly and easily search for trade shows by date, industry, and location. There are trade shows featured from over 45 industries and from over 25 countries.

Figure 4-7 TopTenWholesale's newsroom has a full-time staff that searches for relevant and trending topics in the global sourcing business.

Videos

Clicking on the "Videos" hyperlink brings you to TopTenWholesale.com TV, which is the only video hub dedicated to the wholesale industry. As shown in Figure 4-8, you can either search for videos in the upper left-hand corner or scroll down and search for videos from six different categories. These categories include Most Popular, Newest, Trade Shows, Wholesale, Global Trade, and Marketing. This is a fast and simple way to stay up to date on the latest changes and happenings in the industry.

The amount of free learning in this section of the site is endless. You can watch videos that recap what went on at trade shows (which is especially useful if you weren't able to attend) and/or watch videos with quick and practical advice about how to drop ship. This resource is also a smart way to vet suppliers and learn more about their products. Watch the videos suppliers post to see what products they have or what their production facilities look like.

Figure 4-8 TopTenWholesale.com TV is the only video hub dedicated to the wholesale industry.

Uploading your own business's videos on TopTenWholesale.com also helps to build credibility and more thoroughly introduces you to peers and sourcing partners. To upload a video, go to the "Upload Now" button in the upper right-hand corner of the screen just below the search bar (as shown in Figure 4-8). Once you click on this hyperlink, upload the video and type in its title and description. It's that simple! As a final step, you can choose the channel on which you want the video to be found. Selecting a channel for your videos helps other members of the TopTenWholesale.com community find them more easily. Once you are finished, your video will be accessible to over 500,000 merchandise resellers each month. This is a great way to promote your business and network with other professionals just like you.

With all that it has to offer, TopTenWholesale.com TV is one of the site's most unique and beneficial tools. Shreyans Parekh, cofounder of Koyal Wholesale, agrees: "The video center is a great tool for international sourcing. You get to see how products can be used in their lifestyle setting before buying them."

Answers

TopTenWholesale.com's Answers page allows you to ask and answer questions about the wholesale and manufacturing process, the sourcing industry, recommended suppliers, and so much more (Figure 4-9). It's a forum where other professionals in the network can quickly help you to find what you're looking for and give you advice. It also can be a great tool for vetting suppliers.

You also can browse the questions that have already been posted; simply type in a keyword in the search bar across the top of the page (as shown in Figure 4-9). You also can scroll down and search by categories or industry. To see the categories and industries available, click on the plus signs located in the Categories or Industries boxes. The Categories drop box is open in Figure 4-9. To close this box and open the Industries drop box, simply click on the white plus sign located in the Industries box in the lower left-hand corner. This will automatically close the other drop box. You can close either of the boxes at any time by clicking on the minus sign that appears when the drop-down menu is open.

Figure 4-9 TopTenWholesale.com's Answers section can help you to get quick answers to your sourcing questions.

If you want to ask or answer questions yourself, you can easily do so by clicking on one of the hyperlinks located just to the right of the Categories box. You have three options here: Browse Questions (another way to look at previously asked questions), Ask a Question, or Answer Questions. Just as I explained in Chapter 2, asking and answering questions build credibility, help you to learn important information for your business, and enable you to network with your peers.

SPEAKING WITH THE EXPERTS

I interviewed Jonathan Prescott, a senior business manager at JP Communications, Inc., who manages the accounts of hundreds of wholesalers. He helps to build successful advertising campaigns and gives clients and users support. Here's what he had to say about TopTen Wholesale.com:

Question: "What do members [buyers] need to know about using TopTenWholesale.com?"

Answer: "Buyers need to know that TopTenWholesale.com is a free tool that helps them source more effectively. From the administrative area, buyers are able to save their favorite suppliers and products, as well as connect directly with some of the largest manufacturers, importers, and distributors in the world.

"Not only do we provide tools that help buyers source, but also suppliers and importers use the TopTenWholesale.com admin to source more securely, safely, and effectively. The most important thing that buyers need to be aware of when using our site is that some of our suppliers are verified, and free members are not. Doing business with a verified member is much more trustworthy and transparent, while doing business with a free member involves more risks."

Question: "How do you help people navigate easily through the site?"

Answer: "I tell buyers to be specific. The more specific they are about the product and supplier they're looking for, the better the results they will get. Buyers also need to know that they can either source by product or supplier type. If the buyer doesn't know exactly what they want, they should search for supplier categories. If the buyer knows what products they want, they should search by product type. Additionally, it's important for buyers to remember that they're connecting directly with suppliers and not buying any product through us."

(continued)

Question: "With so many suppliers using the site, searches can yield a large number of results. What are the best ways to narrow down your search results?"

Answer: "The Categories search feature [listed to the left-hand side of the homepage] makes narrowing down search results simple. There are a few different ways that buyers can narrow search results. First of all, buyers need to be as specific as possible. They'll receive more accurate search results if they are specific about what they're searching for. Secondly, buyers can sort results by region. If the buyer wants to buy from a specific location, they can narrow the results to suppliers from that location, and all suppliers that aren't relevant will be eliminated from the search."

Question: "Aside from your awesome search engine, what are some of the best features on your site and why?"

Answer: "There are so many great features on TopTenWholesale. com! My favorite features (apart from all the great suppliers and products available) include

- "TopTenWholesale News: www.toptenwholesale.com/news/. This is where we have a dedicated team that discusses the most relevant and current industry information and technology. We also have a special section (Company Profiles) that announces new suppliers on TopTenWholesale.com and discusses why these suppliers stand out among their competitors.
- "Top Ten Wholesale TV: www.toptenwholesale.com/wholesale-videos/. Here we allow suppliers to post videos about their companies and products. It's one of my favorites because we were the first to launch such an amazing tool dedicated to allowing suppliers to post their own videos. Videos can really help to create trust and transparency for suppliers and buyers, and it's one of our most popular pages on TopTenWholesale.com.
- "The Buyers Sourcing Page: www.toptenwholesale.com/sourcing. This is my second-favorite page on the site. Here

buyers post the products they're looking for, and we match them with suppliers who contact the buyer directly. This tool helps buyers quickly source from multiple suppliers and get multiple quotes. Also, having suppliers contact the buyer directly frees up time for buyers. They don't have to spend it searching for hard-to-find products."

Question: "Are there any strategies or insider tips for successfully using your site that people don't often come up with on their own?"

Answer: "Be active. We have so many tools that help connect buyers and suppliers instantaneously. Examples are trade chat (allows buyers and suppliers to instant message each other), buy leads (allows suppliers to contact buyers that are looking for products right away), and much more. Also, as a supplier, the more time you spend uploading products, adding videos, and making sure your listings are online, the more trust you create, which, in turn, will create more business."

Question: "What is your favorite part about working with customers?"

Answer: "I often take for granted how many secrets I know about this industry and all the knowledge I have about manufacturers, importers, and distributors. When I help make that perfect connection or help a buyer learn the first steps to sourcing online, I get to feel the satisfaction that we have such a great product that truly helps buyers and sellers."

Question: "What else do you want new buyers to be aware of?"

Answer: "Always make sure that you do your due diligence when sourcing. Whether vetting a verified member or a free member, always get reviews, ask for a few referrals, and make sure you have several different suppliers to choose from, just in case your main supplier can't get you what you need."

Contact Supplier and Trade Chat

Remember when I said that registering on TopTenWholesale.com would help you to contact suppliers more easily? Well, here's how. If you find a supplier that you want to contact right away during your search (and you're registered), the Contact Supplier and Trade Chat tools are accessible through your search results. When you click on the "Contact Supplier" button (which features the "mail" symbol), you'll land on a page that's set up just like e-mail (shown in Figure 4-10). This e-mail message allows you to contact the supplier directly and immediately inquire about the product that you are looking for.

Send Supplier a Message

From:	Dolores Lee
To:	**Via Trading Sales**, Via Trading Corporation
Subject: *	Plain White Tee-Shirts
Message: *	Hi there, I am looking for 500x high quality cotton plain white tee-shirts in all different sizes.

2901 characters remaining (English only)

Send Message

Your contact information will be shared with the recipient of this message. Click here to make sure your information is correct.

Warning: False inquiries, solicitations or spam messages will result in cancellation of your membership.

Figure 4-10 Clicking on the "Contact Supplier" button allows you to quickly and easily e-mail suppliers and inquire about their products.

Perhaps you want to speak directly with a supplier and ask some questions immediately. If this is the case, Trade Chat is the best option for you. Trade Chat is a free and secure messaging system that allows you to communicate in real time with suppliers. You can see who is online, get product quotes, and send suppliers images of the product you're looking for. To use this feature, click on "Trade Chat" (with the "globe" logo), and you are taken to a live instant-messaging screen. You'll be marveled by how instantaneous it truly is!

When I tested out Trade Chat while writing this, the administrator, Jordan Xiong, from the wholesale and closeout company Global

Imports, Inc., immediately wrote, "Hi, how may I help you?" This tool truly proves to be fast and effective! Skip McGrath, online selling expert and coach, agrees that this is his favorite tool on TopTenWholesale.com:

> The chat tool is very useful because you get answers right away. I am a big fan of TopTenWholesale.com, and I use it all the time. Tools like this make it such a helpful platform for small to medium sellers like me.

Managing Your Account

When I first got you registered, I listed some of the tools available in the Managing Your Account section, but now let's go back and look at a couple more of the handy tools available in this section. From no matter where you are exploring on the site, you can always click on the "Manage Account" hyperlink, and you will be taken to your own personal administrative hub. The hyperlink is located at the very top to the middle right of every screen within TopTenWholesale.com. Click on this link any time you want to see messages from suppliers, update your company profile, make product requests, and more.

One important part of this administrative center is your Dashboard. The Dashboard is like your own personal homepage. Here you can get quick updates about what's taking place in all aspects of your supplier searches and sourcing information hunts. An extremely useful tool available within the Dashboard is the Quick Menu located to the left of the screen. You'll see five hyperlinks located in the Quick Menu. Let's look at two of the most important and useful features from the Quick Menu now.

Add Product Alert

When you click on the hyperlink "Add Product Alert," you go to the page shown in Figure 4-11. Creating a product alert allows you to receive e-mail updates related to the items that you're looking to source. You'll be notified when suppliers list items that match the merchandise in your Product Alert. All you have to do is customize your alert settings by filling out the product type, your e-mail address, the format in which you want to receive the alert (html or text), and how often you want to receive the product alert e-mails (daily, weekly, or twice a week). Then click the "Add Product Alert" box, and you are done. The TopTen Wholesale.com site and team will now act as your very own personal matchmaker, setting you up with the best suppliers in the industry.

Figure 4-11 shows a sample Product Alert below the customization settings in the Add New Alert section. This sample alert is set up for shoes. As you can see, an alert contains a picture of the item, its description, the price of the item, where the supplier is located, and whether or not the supplier is a verified Supplier Pass or Premium Member. You also have the ability to contact the supplier if you wish.

Additionally, the alert helps you to easily find other suppliers with similar items. Click on the "Products Like This" hyperlink below, and you will receive listings from different suppliers with similar products. You can examine these listings to ensure that you are getting the best deals, products, and prices. All the benefits of the Product Alert feature couldn't make the sourcing process any easier!

Custom Product Request

Now go back to your Dashboard and find the Quick Menu again. Just under the "Add Product Alert" hyperlink there is a "Post a Product Request" hyperlink. Click here, and you will see a blank version of Figure 4-12. The Product Request feature allows you to request specific products from suppliers. This is especially helpful when you want to manufacture a unique product of your own with a supplier overseas or when you are searching for a specific or hard-to-find product.

To fill out the product request, start with the product name, category, and details. Then attach photos, drawings, specification sheets, or other relevant documents that help suppliers better understand your product requirements. As a final step, specify the order quantity and the end date by which you are willing to receive potential suppliers' replies to your request. You also can add in your business type and website URL if you wish. Once you press the blue "Submit Request" button at the bottom of the screen, TopTenWholesale.com will go out and find potential suppli-

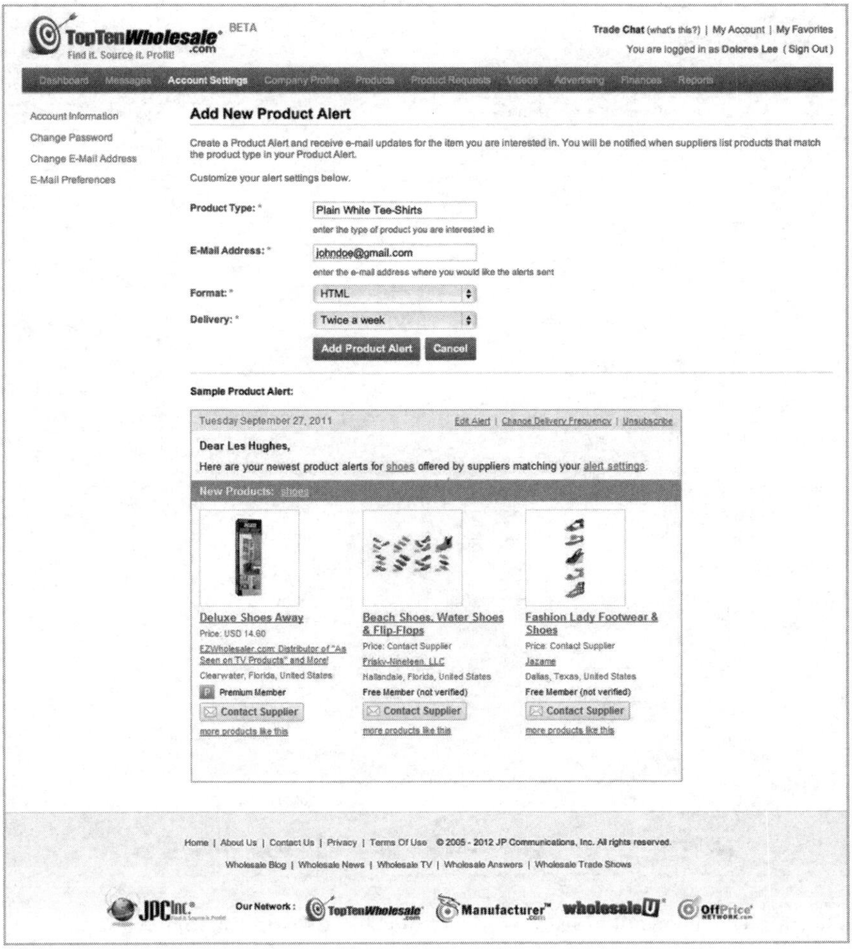

Figure 4-11 Creating a product alert allows you to receive listings for suppliers who have the products that you're looking to source.

ers for you. I highly recommend attaching drawings or pictures to your request because they help you to get the most relevant responses from the best suppliers. Talia Goldfarb, cofounder of Myself Belts, agrees: "Sending suppliers as many pictures and drawings as you can helps them understand exactly what you're looking for."

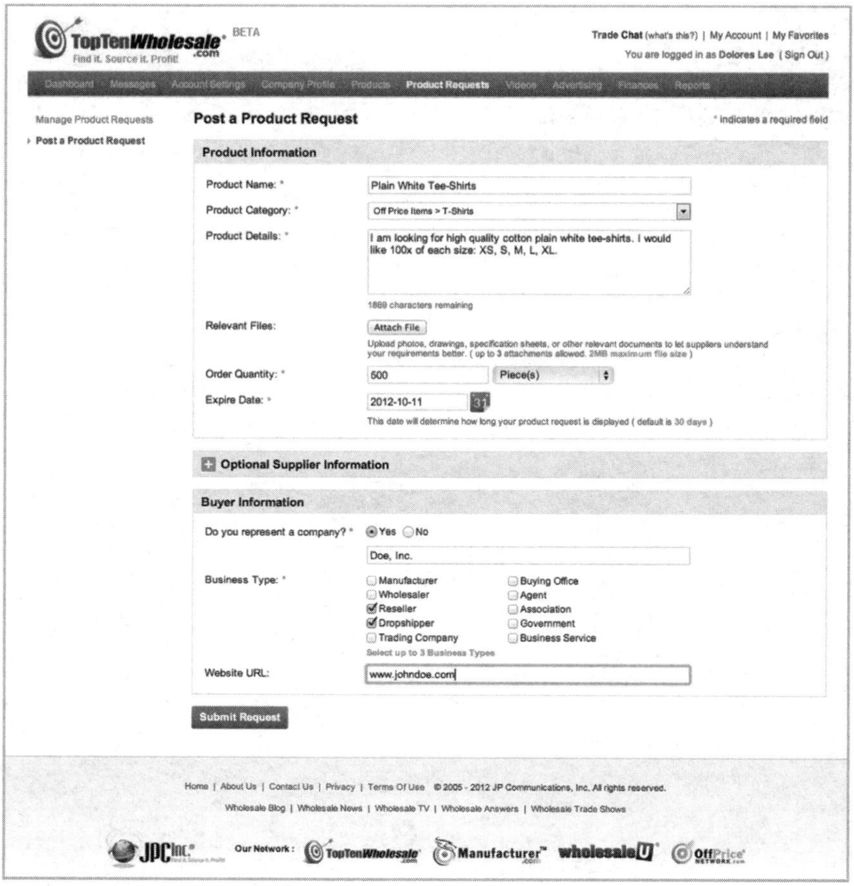

Figure 4-12 Filling out a custom product request can help you to find a supplier that will make your unique products (don't forget to include drawings).

TIP

When sending an RFQ or product request form to suppliers, you should look for 10 to 20 suppliers with whom you would like to work. Some of them may offer similar products, but of the 20, there could be five or six that offer something different. Having these five or six options with distinctive offerings could be what makes the difference in finding the perfect supplier for you.

Additional Services: Trade Managers and Sourcing Trips

TopTenWholesale.com also offers you the ability to call its trade managers at any time. They can help you with everything from recommending suppliers to placing an order or give you advice about what trade show would be best for you to attend. This service is free of charge, so why not take advantage of getting expert advice?

SUPPLIER'S PERSPECTIVE: WHY YOU WILL FIND THE BEST SUPPLIERS ON TOPTENWHOLESALE.COM

I asked the owner of Kole Imports, Rob Kole, why suppliers are bringing their businesses online and investing in marketing and advertising through B2B platforms such as TopTenWholesale.com. Here's what he had to say:

Question: "How much of your business is based online versus when you first started the business?"

Answer: "It's grown by 30 percent."

Question: "What do you think has caused this growth?"

Answer: "Buyers have become more comfortable with purchasing online, and we have become more adept at selling online."

Question: "How much more significant do you feel trade platforms will be over the next five years for your business?"

Answer: "Trade platforms will become extremely more significant."

Question: "How much money are you investing today in online marketing and media versus when you first started the business?"

Answer: "We are investing 10 times as much in online marketing and media than when we first started the business."

Question: "How has TopTenWholesale.com helped your business, and why would you recommend its services?"

Answer: "TopTenWholesale.com is a great source of connecting buyers with suppliers, and I would highly recommend it to anyone looking to grow their business."

The site also does custom sourcing trips. It can either arrange for you to meet a personal guide overseas who will show you around various factories or simply set up appointments for you to visit a couple factories on your own. Either way, the site rarely charges for these services. It's the duty of the site to make sure that you have the ability to connect with suppliers.

I would like to note that when this book was being written, we were under a major revamp of Manufacturer.com. Manufacturer.com was officially re-released in March 2013 at the ASD Trade Show in Las Vegas. Many of the features on Manufacturer.com are similar to TopTenWholesale.com. Some major additions that you will notice right away are our Made In the USA zone and access to manufacturers, exporters, and businesses in over 190 countries. Manufacturer.com aims to be the largest global trade platform in the world—headquartered in the United States.

Conclusion

Now that you are familiar with the perks of sourcing online with B2B trade platforms and the ins and outs of the features on TopTenWholesale.com, you are so much closer to finding the right suppliers for your business. You know how to safely vet potential trading partners from the start, and you have insider strategies for finding the best suppliers available. You understand why B2B platforms make your life easier when it comes to sourcing, and you are aware of how to take advantage of the tools that these types of sites offer. You're well on your way to achieving sourcing success!

Looking Ahead

In Chapter 5, I'll discuss all there is to know about trade shows. You will learn how to find the perfect trade shows for your business and understand all the benefits that the best shows out there can offer you. You'll also gain insider strategies for working and navigating these shows.

5

Trade Shows: Where Do I Go?

It is not often that a man can make opportunities for himself.
But he can put himself in such shape that when or if the
opportunities come, he is ready.

—*Theodore Roosevelt (1858–1919), 26th U.S. President*

IN CHAPTER 4 you learned about sourcing online. Now you are familiar with your trusty allies TopTenWholesale.com and Manufacturer.
com and how to effectively and safely navigate through these types of
sites. Now that you understand how to source online and the resources
and benefits that doing so offers, you are ready to look at trade shows.

The Value of Finding the Right Show

Online business-to-business (B2B) platforms for finding wholesalers
and manufacturers, such as TopTenWholesale.com and Manufacturer.
com, may be your first stop for locating new global and domestic trade,
but once you have made some contacts, it's a good idea to spend some
face-to-face time getting to know the people with whom you may be
working. The opportunities to meet important industry colleagues are
just one of the unique competitive advantages that trade shows offer. By
attending, you also gain the ability to discover the latest products, inno-

vations, and trends; pit suppliers against each other to receive the best deals or request for quotations (RFQs); conduct competitive research; touch base with your suppliers and get to know their staff; find backup suppliers; spark your imagination for new methods of sourcing; and make invaluable connections with key players in the industry.

• • •

Trade shows are events, categorized by industry, where important players meet to exhibit products, learn about current industry trends, and network with people in their profession. Although trade shows are invaluable and indispensable venues, they can be a bit overwhelming—especially mammoth shows such as the ASD Trade Show, the MAGIC Trade Show, the Consumer Electronics Show (CES), and the National Hardware Show. And these are just the domestic shows. If you venture outside the United States, you can't forget about the Canton Fair or the Yiwu International Commodities Fair, where differences in language and culture make keeping your focus that much more difficult.

However, trade shows will provide education, training, and networking that open doors to knowledge. There are so many opportunities to learn more about your industry at these shows, and better yet, with the insider tips I'll share with you, suppliers will fight for your business. You'll have the knowledge you need to negotiate favorable terms with minimal risk. You'll learn how to use meeting time wisely to get key questions answered and maneuver through the shows with ease. From there you can bargain for the best prices, terms, and services, which will eventually lead to higher profitability. To make the benefits of attending shows more clear, let's look at the top eight reasons to attend trade shows.

Top Eight Reasons to Attend Trade Shows

1. *Trade shows allow you to create and develop relationships with new trading partners.* The shows offer you an opportunity to meet with sourcing partners face to face. If your supplier is from overseas, this is an especially invaluable opportunity to develop a more personal

relationship. The time you spend together creates bonds that run deeper than electronic exchanges, such as e-mailing back and forth or just surfing a business's website.

2. *Trade shows allow you to become an information magnet.* You can gather new leads, contacts, catalogues, business cards, and personal impressions of potential partners. This information can help you to evaluate new sourcing partners.

3. *Trade shows allow you to attend conferences, seminars, and networking events.* These events broaden your imagination and open your business to new distribution and marketing tactics. They expose you to some of the most important experts in your industry and allow you to delve into the hot industry topics and trends. And who knows, you may meet your next sourcing partner there. I recently gave a seminar at an ASD Trade Show with someone who had been a buyer for Walmart. The seminar was on strategies for selling to big-box retailers (get ready for some of these essential tips in Chapter 6). Although you can watch the video, there is no way to supplement the questions and answers session that happened afterward. This is a great opportunity to speak with the expert panelists in person.

4. *Trade shows allow you to work your way to the top of the supply chain.* You can discover the most important distributors, importers, wholesalers, and manufacturers and allow them to compete for your business. Having so many potential partners in the same space allows you to get a transparent view of the products and prices in the market. Also, by playing the field, you give yourself many opportunities to get the best deal and make suppliers work to win your business.

5. *Trade shows allow you to explore the differences in working with international versus domestic suppliers.* Most trade shows have international sourcing areas where you can meet, for example, with factory reps; this is a great alternative to a trip to China or India (and a bit less expensive, too). Exhibit areas such as these allow you to meet current or potential trading partners face to face and understand how they run their businesses.

6. *Trade shows allow you to discover the latest trends.* Trade-show organizers have lots of ways to help people discover innovative products,
including awards ceremonies and special exhibits. The shows allow
you to become immersed in industry happenings. Simply walking by
the booths allows you to see which products are being pushed, copied,
and improved upon. You will find the products that people are running down the aisles to see and understand what consumers want.

7. *Trade shows allow you to make invaluable contacts.* The face-to-
face time that you receive by attending trade shows is priceless. It
allows you to make connections and get to know the people you
already work with or those with whom you would like to work.
Just looking in peoples' eyes, saying hello, and shaking their hands
can give you a lot of information about who they are and how they
do business. Bruce Rubin, partner at Nenko Advisors International,
explains that "you gotta see the whites of their eyes and they gotta
see the whites of yours." Getting to know your supplier in person
helps you to do business and interact with them more successfully.
After all, much of business is about trust and going with your gut.
Being face to face with suppliers gives your intuition signals as to
who could become a great trading partner for years to come.

8. *Trade shows allow you to stimulate your mind and have a blast!* With
all the exhibits, conferences, networking opportunities, and more,
there's no way the energy of the place can't rub off on you.

• • •

How to Find the Right Trade Shows

There are literally thousands of trade shows in the United States alone,
so how do you determine which show is right for you? Later on in this
chapter I will make things pretty simple by giving you a rundown on
the shows that I feel are most important for you to consider. However,
I will only be covering the consumer-merchandise sector, so read on to
learn how to do your own comprehensive searching.

TIP

One great way to search for trade shows is by visiting TopTenWhole sale.com's trade-show database at www.toptenwholesale.com/ tradeshows/.

Choosing the right trade show comes down to finding the shows that have the products you are looking for and that cater to your industry.

When looking for trade shows, you also need to keep in mind the type of supplier that you're looking for. Refer back to Chapter 3 if you need a refresher. If not, you are ready to start your search.

A good way to find trade shows is by asking your industry partners and peers which shows they attend. You can meet retailers that sell similar products to you by attending industry-networking events that you find on LinkedIn or Meetup.com. These events present you with great opportunities to ask your industry colleagues questions. At these events, peers can share advice not only on what shows to attend but also on what suppliers they work with. You also can ask potential supplier partners or suppliers that you already work with where they go. Understanding which shows they attend (and why) gives you insight into where other suppliers with similar goods will be.

Once you have spoken to industry partners and peers, you should cross-check whether the suggested shows are best for you. You can do this by using trade-show search engines, which give you a comprehensive list of all the shows that exist in your industry. Here are the trade-show search engines that I recommend:

- www.TopTenWholesale.com/tradeshows
- www.tsnn.com (Trade Show News Network)
- www.eventseye.com/
- www.biztradeshows.com/
- www.thetradeshowcalendar.com/

You'll find that these offer not only a database of shows but also content, blogs, news, and videos on respective shows you may want to attend. Each search engine will vary slightly in the shows it features, but they will all allow you to search by specific details such as city, state, country, month, industry, and show name. Searching for shows couldn't be easier!

Nielsen Media, Reed, and Advanstar are other great resources for finding trade shows because they are the major trade-show producers. Their websites always list the trade shows that they sponsor and often list other industry-wide trade shows as well. And *Exhibit City News* is another source worth mentioning. This is a newspaper that covers the trade-show industry and has a great online monthly trade-show calendar: www.exhibitcitynews.com/.

Commercial newswire companies often have trade-show listings on their websites as well. Linda Musgrove, founder and president of Trade-Show Teacher (a results-driven full-service trade-show management firm), recommends Business Wire: www.businesswire.com/portal/site/home/, in her article, "How to Search for Targeted Trade Shows," on www.tsea.org/. Business Wire is a great example of a commercial newswire company that allows you to find trade shows sorted by industry or month. It provides you with websites, news, and press releases organized by trade show, industry, or subject.

Linda's article also recommends your local Chamber of Commerce as another good place to look for trade shows and get loads of useful business information. Chambers of Commerce often host networking events where they announce tabletop expos and semiregional events with neighboring Chambers of Commerce. Here you can showcase products, build contacts in the industry, and find upcoming trade-show schedules. These schedules are also listed on their websites and in their newsletters and flyers.

Additionally, Linda explains that trade-show calendars can be found in visitors' bureaus and convention centers. Many shows are hosted in these locations, and by looking at their directories, you can discover upcoming events. Their websites also have important detailed information about the shows and their surrounding area. Such information can include the show facility, city attractions, good restaurants, transportation information, and so on.

Other good online resources for finding shows are industry-association websites. Industry associations such as the American Apparel and Footwear Association (www.wewear.org) often organize one national or international show in addition to smaller regional events. By looking at the website's event page or trade-show calendar, you can find a ton of places to go and things to do. And don't limit yourself to searching only the websites and trade shows listed by the umbrella organization of your industry. Check out the association's regional chapter sites as well as the subgroups' pages.

• • •

Megy Karydes, president of Karydes Consulting, board member of the Fair Trade Federation, and founder of www.World-Shoppe.com, gives some insider tips to finding international trade shows: "If you are serious about sourcing globally, then a great resource is the consulate office of the country in which you want to work. Sometimes consulate offices have special programs with international trade organizations so that they can connect you with sources and tell you about trade shows happening in the respective country." She further explains that in India there are trade shows that will even pay your way to the show if you are a serious buyer: "If you want to go to India and source apparel, jewelry, or accessories, there are trade shows that actively solicit international buyers and will pay for you to come to their show." Costs they cover include your flight, hotel, and often some other basics for up to three nights. The trade shows do this to get qualified buyers from other countries to come. You also can contact the trade-show organizers directly to see if they have any amenities available for international buyers. And if you are concerned about safety, Megy offers a tip for first-timers traveling to foreign countries: "Have someone on the ground in the country that you are traveling to. Make sure that they know when you're coming, where you're staying, and that they can be your guide while you're there."

How to Narrow Down the Shows You Attend

Now that I've given you several methods for locating trade shows, you are probably wondering how you will choose which show(s) to attend. The following list of questions can help you to evaluate the trade shows you come across:

1. Does the show cater to your industry?
2. What people and organizations typically exhibit at the show?
3. Which shows will your industry peers and/or benchmark be attending?
4. What resources does the show offer that make it worth attending?
5. Is this show better than other shows with similar products and structure?
6. Will there be both domestic and international suppliers?
7. Will the suppliers you already work with or are interested in working with be there?
8. Will the suppliers that attend have minimum-order quantities (MOQs) that meet your buying needs?

This list can help you to quickly evaluate the shows that you encounter with a critical eye. It's also always good to contact trade-show organizers and ask them how many attendees and exhibitors they're expecting at the show. Trade-show websites also may keep a running tally.

TIP

To get a good idea of the types of exhibitors that will be attending a show, ask the trade-show organizers for a copy of last year's exhibitor directory, or check it out on the trade-show's website.

WHOLESALE MARTS AND BUYING DISTRICTS

Although not considered official trade shows, there are many local wholesale markets and districts that are set up like year-round trade shows. If you own a small store and have limited storage space, this may be a good place to start. Most of the larger cities in the United States have these permanent spaces where small resellers can go to buy products anytime. From New York City's wholesale and garment districts, to Dallas's Harry Hines Boulevard, to the Los Angeles wholesale district, there's bound to be a buying Mecca near you. Some important wholesale marts and districts I recommend visiting in North America's major cities include

- America's Mart in Atlanta, GA: www.americasmart.com/
- The Dallas Market Center: /www.dallasmarketcenter.com/
- The World Market Center in Las Vegas, NV: www.wmclv.com/
- The Wholesale District in Los Angeles, CA: http://fashiondistrict .org/ (*Note:* This is a resource for the fashion district, although there are also toy and general-merchandise districts as well.)
- The Miami Merchandise Mart: www.miamimerchandisemart. com/
- Various merchandise and garment districts throughout New York City: www.nyc.com/visitor_guide/garment_district.75853/ editorial_review.aspx
- Midwest Market Days in Chicago, IL: http://midwestmarketdays .com/. (*Note:* Midwest Market Days is more of an ongoing trade show than a mart because it hosts approximately seven events a year. Check out the calendar of events on the website to see if there is a show that is relevant and convenient for you.)

This is not an exhaustive list, so do search for other marts near you. You may find a convenient district close to home with the goods and suppliers you're looking for. Marts are usually a bit smaller than trade shows, so they are a great resource and place to start sourcing.

Trade Show Recommendations, Innovations, and Technology

Now that you know how to find trade shows and choose the ones that meet your needs, let's explore the shows that I consider most important. Because you understand what your business and sourcing needs are, it will be much easier to know which of these trade shows is right for you. And learning about all of them will give you important industry insights.

Below is a list of the trade shows, both domestic and international, that I feel you have to know about—they are that important. Please be aware that I have chosen to focus on the shows that touch the heart of basic consumer needs, not industrial needs. Basic consumer needs include general merchandise, home-ware supplies, hardware, apparel/fashion, and consumer electronics. To find shows outside this scope, please refer to the "How to Find the Right Trade Shows" section earlier. Are you ready? The shows that I feel you must know about are

- ASD
- MAGIC
- National Hardware Show
- Consumer Electronics Show
- International Home and Housewares Show
- Off Price Show
- Yiwu Fair
- Canton Fair
- New York International Gift Fair
- JCK
- Couture

Table 5-1 shares information about who will be there, what industries the shows cater to, when the shows normally take place, where the shows are located, and the trade shows' websites.

Table 5-1   Trade-Show Guide and Dates for Sourcing Success

Show Name	Industry	When	Where	Website
ASD	General merchandise	February/ March, August	Las Vegas, NV; New York City	www.asdonline.com/
SOURCING at MAGIC	Women and men's apparel, footwear, and accessories	February and August	Las Vegas, NV	www.magiconline.com/
National Hardware Show	Hardware and tools	May	Las Vegas, NV	www.nationalhard-ware show.com/
CES	Consumer electronics	January	Las Vegas, NV	http://cesweb.org/
International Home and Housewares Show	Home and garden	March	Chicago, IL	www.house-wares.org/ show/
OffPrice Show	20–70 percent below wholesale clothing, accessories, and footwear	August	Las Vegas, NV	www.offpriceshow.com/
Yiwu Fair	General merchandise	October	Yiwu, Zhejiang Province, China	http://en.chinafairs.org/
Canton Fair	General merchandise	April, October/ November	Guangzhou, China	www.chinacanton-fair.com/
N.Y. International Gift Fair	Middle to high-end gift items for high-scale boutiques	January and August	New York City	www.nyigf.com/Home.aspx
JCK	Jewelry	May, June, July, August, and October	Las Vegas, NV; Toronto, Canada; Panama City, Panama	www.jckonline.com
Couture	Couture jewelry	February and May/June	New York City; Las Vegas, NV	www.national-jeweler.com/cj/

Another show worth visiting is the Internet Retailer Conference and Exposition. This show is held in June in Chicago and is a little different from the other types of shows that I mentioned earlier. It focuses on e-commerce technology and search-engine optimization (SEO). Retailers and business owners from a myriad of industries can attend. The show provides valuable information about how to run an online store and helps you to keep up with the rapidly evolving changes on the Internet.

Don Davis, editor in chief at Internet Retailer, shares some of the benefits of attending this show:

> We organize the agenda into tracks so that attendees can focus on the topics that interest them, whether it's operations, marketing, fulfillment, global selling, or others. We have tracks for small retailers and others for big retailers, ones for retailers with brick-and-mortar stores and for web-only merchants. We also have full-day workshops that focus on specific topics, such as search-engine marketing, mobile commerce, and social media marketing.

Study the schedule in advance, and focus on the topics and exhibitors in which you are most interested. There are hundreds of sessions over four days at IRCE (Internet Retailer Conference and Exposition) and 564 companies exhibiting on the show floor, so it's important that an attendee know what he or she is looking for. Prioritize the sessions and exhibitor meetings that will best suit your needs. For more information, see http://irce.internetretailer.com.

Innovation at Trade Shows

Trade shows are fun, exciting, and inspiring. They keep you up to date on the latest trends and products in your field. The new technology and services that you will encounter there keep you in the know about advances happening in the business and sourcing world. From interesting conferences and events, to international pavilions, to B2B matchmaking services, each show has its own innovative way of catering to your business needs.

John Banker, sales director for ASD, shared some of ASD's most interesting show services:

- Show planners
- Appointment settings
- Exhibitor matching capabilities
- Printable floor plans based on preselected exhibitors and sequence of their booth numbers on the show floor
- Shuttle services
- Merchandise locator/show directories
- Discounts on food, beverage, and entertainment
- Networking events such as official happy hours and opening-night and closing-night parties
- Hotel discounts
- Free airport shuttles on the last day of the show
- Buyer newsletters

All these services have been developed over the years to help make buyers' experiences more satisfying. Many people are not aware of all the services available, so do your research and take advantage of all the savings and offerings.

Spotlight on MAGIC

Karalynn Sprouse, vice president of MAGIC International, gave us the inside scoop on MAGIC (Men's Apparel Guild in California), which is one of the most important trade shows in the apparel industry. She explained how as host to the world's most comprehensive apparel, footwear, and accessories trade event in North America, MAGIC unites influential fashion and retail decision makers and the world's leading and most innovative fashion brands. She further explained that MAGIC inspires the fashion community and connects over 5,000 leading and emerging fashion brands and 20,000 product lines. The show also boasts over 60,000 visitors from more than 80 countries. By looking in depth at MAGIC, I was able to understand what one of the most developed shows in the trade-show industry is doing to help buyers.

The buyers who attend MAGIC shows include key decision makers, big-box/discount retailers, specialty-store retailers, sourcing executives, brands, design, and trend influencers, U.S. and other trade officials from all over the world, and the press. They attend to meet some of the 4,000 exhibitors and to pick from nearly 20,000 product lines at each show. The various sections of the show are broken into the following four categories:

- WWD MAGIC (women's/children's/juniors/accessories/ swim brands)
- FN Platform (women's, men's and children's footwear)
- MAGIC Men's and Street Wear (young men's, licensing, menswear and street/surf/skate wear)
- SOURCING at MAGIC (apparel, accessories, and footwear resources merchandised by country and category)

• • •

Designed for global product sourcing, the SOURCING at MAGIC section of the show is especially useful for my purposes. It hosts nearly 1,000 contract, original design manufacturers (ODMs), and fabric/trim suppliers from over 40 countries. Buyers who attend this show include branded wholesalers, private-label retailers, importers, and distributers looking to manufacture new products and/or buy original designs in large quantities. This section of the show helps to provide global connections for buyers and suppliers that regional or domestically focused shows can't.

The show even has a matchmaking program that provides an onsite resource center with experts who match retailers with exhibitors. The program researches all suppliers attending the show and their products. From this research, the staff develops lists of exhibitors that meet retailers' sourcing needs so that they can navigate the floor in a timely and efficient manner.

• • •

Since February 2012, TopTenWholesale.com and Manufacturer.com have been running the buyer services in the China Pavilion at SOURCING at MAGIC. Buyers can have translators escort them to exhibitors to discuss supplier and product information.

TIP

Before you arrive at MAGIC, set up an appointment with the sourcing center. In this way, an expert will meet with you when you arrive at the show and provide you with a list of the suppliers that best suit your sourcing needs.

A few of MAGIC's other special services include private meeting and conference space at the show, VIP car and hotel reservation services, and niche target mailings that help you to connect with exhibitors. The staff works year round arranging face-to-face visits with buyers, roundtable dinners, new-product launches, and educational programs so that you are plugged into the industry at all times.

Especially interesting as well are the networking and educational programs that assist buyers with navigating the show floor and meeting exhibitors. By using the show's online services in advance, you can map out the show, make appointments with exhibitors, and schedule the educational conferences and networking events you want to attend. To do so, use magiconline.com's online show planner and the MAGIC mobile application. You also can stay current throughout the year with events and new brands/initiatives by visiting the MAGIC Facebook, Twitter, LinkedIn, and Pinterest pages. In addition, at any time you can contact the attendee relations' team to discover what is coming up at the next event.

I also asked Karalynn Sprouse for advice for first-time buyers at MAGIC. She suggests that "talking to industry peers that have attended in the past, and visiting with our attendee relations' team so they can quickly help you understand how to use our buyer services (both preshow and on site) to make the most out of your experience. Set up appointments in advance, but leave yourself plenty of time to discover and pick up charming new resources."

I also suggest that you check out some of the 30 to 40 conferences per show that MAGIC offers. The conferences will help to educate you on topics including updates on international trade policies, key industry influencers, and new digital initiatives.

Technological Innovation at Trade Shows

Smart phones, tablets, and the ubiquity of high speed data connections are helping to fuel a trade show technological revolution. Mobile apps and interactive floor plans are now available at most major events.

GETTING WITH THE TIMES IN TRADE-SHOW TECHNOLOGY

Trade shows are on the cutting edge of technology. Some shows have incorporated blogger lounges, which make products, trends, and even events at the show accessible to those who can't attend. Many trade shows are also starting to create their own mobile applications to help you to navigate while there. One such example is MAGIC's mobile application, which is downloadable at www.magiconline.com/magic-mobile-application. These types of applications help you to stay organized, see your schedule, chime in on social media conversations, locate exhibitors, and connect with colleagues who are attending the show.

Michelle Bruno's webinar, "Tradeshow Technology Trends You Need to Know About," hosted by the Trade Show News Network, introduced me to some other mobile applications worth checking out. These mobile applications are usable at any show and include Banjo, Beep Mo, and Sonar. Each one helps suppliers and buyers to see who is attending the show. You can even ping people before or during the event to see if they'd like to meet up. You are always able to opt out of a meeting if you aren't interested. But who knows, you could meet your next sourcing partner through this innovative technology.

Near-Field Communication (NCF) and Augmented Reality are some other trade-show tools that industry experts expect to see in the digital space. NCF will allow you to register for the show and pay for products through your mobile phone. When implemented, this technology could save you lots of time and energy; which is especially appreciated when you are trying to find those must-see exhibitors at the show.

Augmented Reality is a technology that allows you to see objects, such as trade-show booths, in an enhanced reality through the lens of your mobile phone. You point your phone at the booth, take a picture, and suddenly additional information about the exhibitor appears on your phone. This can help you to quickly investigate more details about suppliers and determine if they are right for you.

To hear the whole webinar and learn more about new technology in the trade-show industry, go to www.tsnn.com/webinars.

Insider Strategies to Getting the Most Out of the Show

You know how to find shows and the benefits that they can offer, but now let's talk about how to make the most out of your attendance at these shows. To have you sailing through them with ease, I have gathered advice from the pros. I have tips for not only what to do during the show but also for what to do before and after the show as well. This information will allow you to reap benefits, including great bargains and deals.

I spoke with Judi Brown, owner of Getting Personal Imprinting, LLC, who shared why it's important to plan ahead and be strategic at trade shows:

> The first show we ever attended was a large general-merchandise show, and it was overwhelming. We went in knowing nothing and really just wanted to look and see what was on display. As it turned out, we traveled out of state, only to make a purchase from a supplier whose operations were based less than 10 miles from where we lived.
>
> At a later show we purchased a piece of equipment that was the first on the market for a new style of printer. We learned an expensive lesson and will not do that again. That particular piece

of equipment worked for a few months, broke down, the supplier went bankrupt, and in the end, we were left with an expensive dust collector.

We're a bit more strategic these days. We generally review the list of expected exhibitors ahead of time and make notes to visit certain suppliers. Some suppliers are people we already do business with, whereas others are companies that look like they offer products we'd like to add to our inventory. We still spend time wandering around the show floor just looking to see what else is there, but we're less inclined to jump at a trade-show pitch.

We've met good and bad supplier reps at these shows. The good ones are those who come across as people who truly want to be a partner and resource to us. They are the ones we connect with on LinkedIn and Facebook and invest our time with to develop the relationship.

What to Do before the Show

Preshow preparation requires the consideration of many details. Some of those details include what to bring, what to wear, where to stay, making a schedule, knowing what product lines you want to see and what exhibitors you want to meet, choosing seminars/events to attend, and more. Many trade shows actually provide you with a preshow checklist such as this one from ASD: www.asdonline.com/lv/attendee/check-list. This list gives you an idea of some of the things you should do before and after the show, such as making notes on your best-selling merchandise before the show, packing your resale certificate and tax ID number, and checking whether the company is licensed in the state in which it is based.

The preshow planning stage is extremely important. It allows you to make the most of your limited time while at the show. Go prepared. Some shows are three to five days long, but you will be surprised at how quickly that time gets away from you. You need to use it wisely. Below I have broken down some essential preshow planning tips to help you arrive ready.

Start by thinking about your goals. Write down a clear set of objectives, and know what you want to get out of the show. Whether it's finding new suppliers or products, scouting out new trends, or gaining knowledge and learning at seminars, stay focused so that you can plan according to your goals.

Another thing to do before the show is preregister on the trade show's website. Preregistering allows you to receive important updates and information. You will avoid attendance fees and save yourself from losing time in lines when you arrive. Furthermore, by preregistering, you gain access to important information about the show and its exhibitors. This also will allow you to see lists of exhibitors and exhibit-hall maps.

Look at the exhibitor directory, and do research about the vendors that are most interesting to you. Professor Dawn Fotopulos, founder of BestSmallBizHelp.com, explains her strategy:

> Get the list of vendors in advance. Narrow down the categories of goods/services you're most interested in. Then go on the websites of those vendors to learn the basics about them: what they do, how long they've been in business, whom they do business with, and their product lines. Create a short list of "must visit" vendors at the show. Then, before the show, ping vendors to let them know you'll be visiting.

I also suggest creating a spreadsheet with the exhibitors that you would like to see. By doing so, you will ensure that you engage with the most important exhibitors and won't be distracted while walking around the show.

Preregistering provides you with great tools, such as maps of the show grounds and exhibit halls. You can see where specific vendors and industry sections are located, and map out how you want to walk the show. Megy Karydes, board member of the Fair Trade Federation, president of Karydes Consulting, and founder of www.World-Shoppe.com, explained that using the trade show's online resources helps you to save time and energy. She recommends planning your schedule with online agendas because it gives you more time to decide when you would

> **TIP**
>
> Make appointments with exhibitors before the show to harness the power of face-to-face time. Having scheduled time helps to ensure that you don't miss out on meeting with any key candidates. You also can plan to see suppliers that you have already sourced from on TopTenWholesale.com or by other online means to strengthen the relationship.

like to meet with vendors, and prelocate their booths on a floor plan. You then can print out the agenda/floor plan and walk strategically down the aisles based on what you have plotted. This helps to save time and protects your feet from needless wandering back and forth. Megy further explained the helpfulness of these tools:

> They are great from a timing perspective. It saves you from running back and forth and from frustrated thinking like, "Oh my God! This is in the 5,000 aisle, and I'm in the 800 aisle! I have to walk back half a mile to get to that exhibitor."

I also discussed preshow planning with Gregory Lok, CEO and founder of Deal Décor. When explaining the preshow planning process he shared that you should

> Be prepared. As a merchant, you need to have a clear understanding of what product categories you are looking to build up. Identify your needs, and identify the vendors that you want to visit in advance. Start the conversations with them before the trade show begins to get the ball rolling. Then, when you meet with them, you can spend more quality time asking them questions that you can't get solid answers to over the phone. Additionally, this allows you to use that time to get to know the contact person (if they are at the booth) that you would be working with on a daily basis.

Knowing your inventory needs and setting a budget are other essential preshow planning practices. Researching inventory and deciding how much you can spend before the show will help you to focus on buying only what you really want and need. In this way, you won't get fooled into special offers, discounts, and deals for products that you don't know how to sell. Instead, you will be able to spend your time looking for such deals within your product categories.

Skip McGrath, online selling expert and online selling coach, spoke with me and emphasized the importance of setting a focus for the show. He suggests that you only look for what you need and concentrate only on products that you have a knack for selling. He explained that sometimes he and his wife go to a show and see things they like, such as a gorgeous purse. However, because they are not focused on selling fashion and accessories, they usually avoid buying such products. Of course, there are exceptions, and he feels that if you see an amazing opportunity, you don't have to limit yourself. In general, though, you should stick to what you know.

Skip also explained that he loves using trade shows to spark creativity and find products that no one else sells. He finds and creates unique product sets, which he says is one of his secrets to success. He gave me an example of how he does this. While at the ASD Trade Show, he found a scorpion bug stick (a 36-inch-long piece of aluminum) that is used to catch scorpions. He had done some research and found that to catch scorpions, you go out in the night with an ultraviolet flashlight and shine it on them. This makes the scorpions glow in the dark and easier to catch. While at the show, Skip found a vendor that sold scorpion sticks, but not the ultraviolet flashlights. So he immediately walked across the aisle to another vendor selling LED flashlights, took one back over to the scorpion stick, and saw that the flashlight fit perfectly on the stick. By marrying two products from different manufacturers, Skip created a new product set.

You may not be in the business of sourcing scorpion sticks, but this strategy can be used for anything from fashion to hardware. As Skip likes to put it, "Be creative while sourcing, but focus on what you know." I recommend being smart like Skip and researching products before the show. This will help to spark ideas, and you will be prepared to create product sets while there.

You also should book your flight and hotel early. Stay close to the venue to save time and money on transportation to and from the show. This is also helpful in case you run out of something important or need to recharge your phone or tablet. I recommend booking at least 60 days in advance to secure the flight and hotel of your choice. Many locations fill up quickly as the opening day of the show approaches.

TIP

Check with the trade-show organizers to see if they have any discounted hotel rooms reserved near the show. Most trade shows will even send you alerts on travel, seminars, and events once you register or create a profile online. As a buyer, you know that we all love bargains!

Jeremy Shepherd, founder and CEO of Pearl Paradise, also shared some preshow advice for attending international shows. If you already have relationships with exhibiting suppliers, you should try to visit them before the show begins. He explained that he does 90 percent of his buying the week prior to a show because this is when suppliers have their full scope of inventory. Jeremy also explained that this is strategic because other buyers have to select from leftover merchandise, whereas you get the first pick. "This is a little-known secret that serious buyers that go to the Hong Kong shows live by."

What to Bring to the Show

You are a few days away from the start of the show. You know your goals, you've booked your hotel with a discounted rate, and you've even set up meetings with suppliers. Now it's time to start packing. But what should you bring? Luckily (for some), you don't want to bring too much. Following are the key items to put into your suitcase:

- *Comfortable clothing (especially shoes).* You will be walking all day, so it's important to make sure that you don't get too hot, feel restricted, or have blisters on your feet. Clothing should be business casual, but keep in mind that you're representing your company.
- *Lip balm and breath mints.* You will be talking to a lot of people, and nothing is worse than feeling uncomfortable or worried about bad breath.
- *A camera.* Bring a camera that allows you to take photos of booths, exhibitors, and interesting products. Photos help you to remember the products, and vendors will stay fresh in your mind. It's always nice to have an extra set of eyes, especially if they have a photographic memory.
- *A digital voice recorder.* Scott Costantino, merchandise manager from Home Trends Catalog/Picket Fence Catalog, explains that you can "dictate your notes into a digital voice recorder. It is much easier than trying to write down all the info you get at a booth, and you can go back and type up your notes from the show at your own pace."
- *Roller bags.* Instead of lugging around a heavy briefcase, I suggest that you bring a roller bag. This allows you to easily collect catalogues, literature, and business cards.
- *Business cards.* Bringing your business cards allows you to avoid filling out registration forms, helps suppliers to get in touch with you, and makes networking with industry peers easy.
- *Sticker-label pages with your address printed on them.* Megy Karydes, member of Fair Trade Federation, president of Karydes Consulting, and founder of www.World-Shoppe.com, explained that she brings a sticker-label page and prints out 30 to 60 labels with her shipping address. "That way, when suppliers ask you where you would like to ship products or materials, you can give them a sticker to put on their mailing form." This helps you to ensure that suppliers have the correct shipping address.
- *Tablet and smart phone.* If you don't have them, I suggest that you make the investment. You can use them to research suppliers while at the show, ping suppliers that you would like to see, and take

pictures (with permission) of products that you are interested in. Besides, with all the technological advancements happening in the trade-show industry (and today's digital age), they're a must!

What to Do during the Show

Here we are—it's finally opening day of the show. It's going to be a long day, so I advise that you eat a good, healthy breakfast. I also recommend arriving 30 minutes early (especially on the first day), so get a good night's rest, wake up early, and let's get going.

One of the most important things you can do is allow yourself plenty of time at the show. Don't arrive on the second day, go the day before it opens and get organized. Sometimes schedules can change several times before the show begins, so double-check agendas the morning of the show, and make sure that your plan is still viable.

You need to take care of yourself. This may sound silly, but don't forget to drink plenty of water, stop for meals, and take quick breaks. You don't want to wear yourself out, so be kind to yourself. Remember, you can communicate with the suppliers that you don't visit at the show later on TopTenWholesale.com and Manufacturer.com.

I also recommend that you speak to the trade-show staff. I'm not talking about customer-service people but about the executives and managers of the show. Look for the people in suits with the nice name badges. Go and ask them questions such as, "Can you tell me who the popular suppliers for x are?" or "How long have you worked here, and what advice can you give me about the show?" Additionally, you can talk with the show's media partners. Media partners usually handle advertising for show exhibitors, and they know the industry well. Most shows also will have pavilions where select partners are featured. These partners typically can offer inside information, tips, and services that can help you to succeed.

You should request that literature, catalogues, and samples be mailed to you so that you don't have to carry everything around during the show. On the other hand, I do recommend picking up extra copies of show directories while there. These directories are as valuable as gold.

> **TIP**
>
> While at the show, pit suppliers against each other. Use the fact that there are hundreds of suppliers selling the same thing to your advantage. Have the catalogue of the competitor to the supplier with whom you are speaking in your hand. Let the supplier see that you have done your homework. It's not necessary (nor is it a good tactic) to lie or try to swindle the supplier into giving you a deal. Just be honest and say, "I've been looking around at a couple of companies, and I like your stuff, but your pricing is a little high." Or perhaps, "After checking out other booths, I don't like your minimum-order policy." On hearing this, the vendor may ask what you were offered by other exhibitors, but don't give him or her that information. Just reply, "I don't want to tell you what your competitors are offering me. I want to hear about your best terms." Saying this keeps you in control and encourages the supplier to fight for your business.

They list all attending exhibitors and give you options to reference when looking for suppliers.

Another important thing to remember is to attend interesting conferences and events. There are so many learning opportunities at trade shows, and their events are designed to help you stay in the vanguard of the industry. Furthermore, these events are a great opportunity for networking and exploring your peers' solutions to sourcing challenges.

Talia Goldfarb, cofounder of Myself Belts, explains why speaking with peers at trade shows is so important:

We use trade shows to keep our eyes out for trends and inspiration. But the best thing about them is the ability to learn from your peers' experiences. You can hear about great importers, get referrals, and learn from challenges that other vendors are going through. For business owners, trade shows are like going to college.

International Organizers at Trade Shows

When focusing on international sourcing at a trade show, it's important to remember that an organizer sets up the international zones. This person has a lot of insider information. International pavilions often have 30 to 40 booths, and the organizer of these zones knows the suppliers from each of them. This person is a great resource. To find an organizer, ask suppliers at the booths to introduce you to one. Then you can ask the organizer which factories he or she recommends. Organizers can quickly help you figure out who the best suppliers are.

TIP

TopTenWholesale.com is an international organizer for trade shows such as the ASD Trade Show. Many organizers, like TopTenWhole sale.com and Manufacturer.com, will offer trade assistance. They can assign you a trade manager who helps you with communication issues and guides you through your sourcing requests.

Michael Fan, CEO of New Times, gave us the full scoop about what international organizers do. Michael explained that as an international organizer, his company interlinks manufacturers and trading companies in China to over 100 worldwide trade-show exhibitions. New Times builds relationships with trade-show organizers and institutions and recommends the top trade fairs in different countries to Chinese manufacturers. Some of the shows that New Times organizes include CES (www.cesweb.org), IFA (www.ifa-berlin.de), CEBIT (www.cebit.com), CTIA (www.ctiawireless.com), ASD/AMD (www.asdonline.com), HIS (www.ihs.com), and the National Hardware Show (www.nationalhard wareshow.com).

New Times attempts to give small to medium-sized businesses a one-stop shop that connects buyers with suppliers. The company evaluates suppliers and matches them with the best trade shows and exhibiting locations. It gives manufacturers the ability to be independent exhibitors or participate in trade-show associations and national pavilions.

New Times is useful for buyers (wholesalers/retailers) because it knows the location of all the manufacturers at the shows, as well as suppliers' latest products and manufacturing capabilities. Furthermore, New Times teaches exhibitors about the business and cultural practices from the region where the show takes place. This makes communication and transactions easier. Once New Times has prepared exhibitors for the shows, TopTenWholesale.com and Manufactuer.com round up product information from suppliers. Potential buyers then can be matched with suppliers before the show even begins.

Michael further explained why working with TopTenWholesale.com and international organizers is so important:

> Finding a supplier with production capabilities is easy; finding someone who is suitable for you is difficult. In China, it is complicated to find a trustworthy supplier because of ambiguous government policies, an abundance of competition between manufacturers with similar products, and the aggressive state of mind of the people in this industry. You need to work with people who have experience working in both the United States and China.

Michael feels that it's imperative to have a team like TopTenWholesale.com and Manufacturer.com working with a company like New Times. Together they help you thoroughly evaluate suppliers and ensure that they're the perfect partners for you.

Vetting International Suppliers While at Shows

To further verify that suppliers are experienced, be sure that they are familiar with the certifications you need for the products you're sourcing (more on this in Chapter 7). If you still feel uncertain, Michael urges you to see if the supplier has a verified Supplier Pass on TopTenWholesale.com or another B2B trade platform. This helps to prove that the company has been evaluated by a trustworthy source. He also encourages buyers to take advantage of the face-to-face networking opportunities that trade shows present to build relationships with potential or existing partners.

TIP

Michael Fan also gave me some tips for vetting international suppliers while at shows. He explained that you should examine the price quote they give you. If it's in a normal range, they are most likely an experienced exporter. You also should ask them about their competitors' products. If the supplier is serious, he or she will know details about the competitors and be able to explain why his or her products are a better choice.

What to Do When Nearing the End of the Show

Professor Dawn Fotopulos, founder of BestSmallBizHelp.com, advises what to do when the show is nearly over: "On the last day of the show, many vendors like to deep discount the samples they've brought with them so they don't have to ship them back to their warehouses. I always like to stay until the end to get the bargains; they're always there!

Jeremy Shepherd, founder and CEO of Pearl Paradise, agrees:

> By the end of the show, the real deals start happening. If the show has been bad [in terms of sales for the supplier], the vendors will be desperate to do business. If they come from another country with strong import restrictions (such as China), they may feel as though they need to move their remaining inventory before they head home.

However, I don't always recommend that you buy while at a show. Frequently, discounts continue after the show is over. John Banker, ASD sales director, explained that vendors often have special show discounts with a one- or two-week postshow window. Giving yourself time allows you to investigate more about these vendors and products. However, if you find an outstanding deal and/or the product is limited, Dawn and Jeremy's advice is key.

I recommend that you leave the show 20 to 30 minutes early to avoid lines and allow yourself time to make notes about the suppliers you liked. You can make detailed notes in the exhibitor directory about the suppliers that are important to you. Leaving early also gives you time to organize the next day.

USING CAUTION DURING TRADE SHOWS

Trade shows are generally safe events. However, it's always good to use caution when dealing with new people and businesses. In order to help you feel secure, I have broken down some of the key safety tips for both international and domestic shows.

Let's start with international shows such as the Canton Fair or Yiwu Fair in China. These shows can be very overwhelming the first time, so it's good to go prepared. Here are some pointers for staying safe while there:

1. *Stay inside the trade show.* Don't visit factories with people you don't know. Any special deal that a company can offer you should be available on the trade-show site.
2. *Have an interpreter with you.* If you go to a trade show in China, for example, 99 percent of the population doesn't speak English. Some vendors may have basic English skills, but to avoid confusion and bargain for the best deals, I recommend that you hire a translator.
3. *Do not carry excessive amounts of cash.* This is advisable in any big city, but when you are a foreigner in another country, it becomes more important because tourists are often targets for robbery.

(continued)

4. *Read trade-show invitation guides.* Many international trade shows will create guides with safety tips for foreigners. Here's an example of the type of guide I'm referring to: Chinese Canton Fair: http://invitation.cantonfair.org.cn/hows_en/index.html.

5. If an unfortunate accident takes place, always have the emergency number of the country that you are in on hand, and call the police.

Feeling safe at a domestic show is often easier than at an international show. You usually don't have to deal with the added stress of language barriers and cultural differences. Also, you can rest assured that most of the exhibitors at domestic shows are credible. Normally, they have spent a lot of money and time to be able to exhibit there. Nevertheless, this comfort should not leave you with your guard down. You always need to be on the lookout for scams.

Here are some tips to prepare you to spot fraud and incapable suppliers:

1. Ask exhibitors about past shows they have attended. If they have knowledge and experience in attending trade shows, they are less likely to be fraudulent.

2. Hang around vendors' booths. You can ask other booth visitors if they have bought from or are familiar with the suppliers, and you can inquire about their experience doing business with them.

3. Order slowly. If you're feeling unsure about a supplier, it's best to wait and buy after investigating the company at home. You can always use the helpful online resources I recommended earlier: RipoffReport.com, Complaintsboard.com, TopTenWholesale.com, WholsaleU.com, and the Better Business Bureau (BBB).

4. Ask suppliers about their payment terms. Do they work on a letter of credit? Do they take credit cards? Back away if they only take cash and money orders or are demanding a wire transfer up front for the merchandise.

5. Find out if the suppliers advertise in trading magazines or B2B trade sites such as TopTenWholesale.com. If they don't, ask why.

What to Do after the Show

Due diligence also continues once the show is over. One of the most important things to research is the price of the items you want to buy. Call various suppliers and recheck the quotes from 5 to 15 different sources to ensure that you're getting the best price. Then follow up with suppliers as soon as you are ready to buy so that hot or hard-to-find items don't sell out.

However, Bruce Rubin, partner at Nenko Advisors International, explains that if you don't get a reply right away, you shouldn't get frustrated:

> Typically, exhibitors are very busy after the show. It is usually a good idea to wait anywhere from a few days to a week to contact them. In this way, you are not one of the hundreds of people trying to reach them at the same time. You can still send an e-mail to make the contact, but remember that they might not see it right away. Just keep following up until you get an answer.

Insider Advice for Getting Deals after the Show
Nicole Leinbach Reyhle, founder and editorial director of the retail lifestyle publication *Retail Minded* shares an exclusive insider look at what to do when the trade show is over. She especially provides great insider tips about getting bargains after the show:

> When attending a trade show, many retailers fail to plan for the follow-up necessary once a trade show is over. While on-site participation is a critical component in leveraging the opportunities trade shows present, the steps following the show are just as important for retailers.
>
> To begin your follow-up plan of attack, identify your immediate goals. If getting orders placed is on your list, consider which vendors may be either (1) most pressed for time and (2) most challenging to connect with. This is whom you should plan to follow up with first. Typically, it's good to wait three to five days after

the last day of the show. There are a variety of factors that can influence who to contact first, but among them may be trending products, shipping logistics, fulfillment needs, and your store's unique goals.

When connecting with vendors that you met at a trade show, be sure to identify your connection. Remind vendors (who see hundreds or possibly thousands of retailers at each show) where you met them, and they will be more likely to offer you show specials. Vendors often offer incentives for retailers to buy while at the show, yet they know that not all buyers will use them while there. If you fall into this category, let them know up front that you expect any incentives offered at the show to be honored for purchases you make. If they say no to this, politely end the conversation. However, provide them with your contact details first so that they can get in touch should they change their mind. It's very likely they will. And you can make the next move if they don't. Wait a day, call back, and ask them if they are willing to accommodate your requests. Most vendors have some wiggle room in their pricing, so be sure to stay strong in your desired pricing requests. You need to be realistic, but so do they. Together you should be able to work out a reduced price or show special.

For vendors who do not offer show incentives, it's important to consider how else you can save a few bucks. You can request free shipping, extended payment terms, or promotional giveaways to provide to customers. Take the time to discuss unique opportunities with your vendors, letting them know that you need something more than just a flat order with no incentives attached. They will likely respond to your request, knowing that they have to give something to get something.

Finally, remember that vendors will be doing their own follow-up work as well after shows. If you beat them to the punch and get in touch first, they will appreciate your support, enthusiasm, and efficiency. These reasons alone should be enough to get them to accommodate your requests.

Conclusion

Now you understand the value of attending trade shows. You also know how to find the best ones to attend, the innovation and technology they have to offer, and insider strategies to getting the most out of the show. Remember, choosing the right trade show comes down to the products and suppliers you are looking for. Trade shows are well worth the time and effort they require because they offer you invaluable networking and learning opportunities—not to mention the chance to meet lifetime business partners and receive deals not otherwise available to you.

Looking Ahead

In Chapter 6, I will be discussing the many options you have for getting help in analyzing and expertly working with wholesalers and manufacturers, especially those located in other countries, such as China and India. This is how trading companies, which serve as intermediaries between manufacturers and importers, came to be. I will be giving you insider tips not only for working with trading companies but also for working successfully with manufacturers' reps and drop shippers.

6

Working with Trading Companies, Manufacturers' Reps, and Suppliers That Drop Ship

If you have knowledge, let others light their candles in it.

—Margaret Fuller (1810–1850), journalist,
critic, women's rights activist

IN CHAPTER 5, you learned the importance of attending trade shows. You've heard from experts who provided insider advice for getting the most from your time at shows, and I gave you a glimpse at the new technology emerging at these events. You're familiar with the benefits of trade-show seminars and the many resources available to help you to meet trading partners. Moreover, you understand how to get great deals on the merchandise that you find while there.

Now let's discuss working with trading companies, manufacturers' reps, and suppliers that drop ship. Just as with trade shows and business-to-business (B2B) platforms, choosing the right trading companies, manufacturers' reps, and suppliers that drop ship starts with the products and suppliers you're looking for. Different people within these entities will cater to specific product and sourcing niches. You'll want to choose the partners who are experts in your industry and who cater to your specific sourcing needs. Working with each of these resources is different, and knowing which to use and how they work can help you to source the products you want. For example, sometimes you need help when working with overseas suppliers or domestic suppliers with large minimum-order quantities (MOQs). Assisting others is how many of these various entities came to be. They act as intermediaries, helping people like you source from manufacturers or wholesalers that have an MOQ that is too high.

Throughout this chapter, I'll give you tips for working with manufacturers and suppliers that sell to you through trading companies and manufacturers' reps. I'll cover the ins and outs of working with these companies and explain how they can help you to work with suppliers located overseas. In addition, I'll explain how to work with suppliers that drop ship. Let's look at each of these topics in depth now.

Definitions of Trading Companies, Manufacturers' Reps, and Drop Shippers

To get started, let's define each of these sourcing diversification resources to help you become familiar with these terms:

- *Trading companies.* Trading companies serve as intermediaries between manufacturers and importers. Ralph Deng, CEO of the trading company China East Star Holding Group, explains the functions and services that trading companies offer:

  Trading companies play an import role in the supply chain. They're like a bridge that is connected with suppliers on one side and the buyers of the goods on the other. Trading companies are important because they create opportunities for buyers through the relationships they have with suppliers. Services they can provide to buyers include product inquiries, price quotes, order placement, production follow-up, commodity inspections, customs declarations, customs inspections, transportation, distribution, and payments.

It's also important to note that there are two types of trading companies. The first type will act as a middleman, handling management, payment, and other logistical issues related to the merchandise for the buyer, whereas the second type will act as a broker and connect the buyer directly with the manufacturer. They will charge the factory a commission for the connection, but they'll let the buyer and seller maintain the relationship without getting involved. The second type of trading company, which only provides the connection, is much less common because the most coveted thing a trading company has are its relationships with factories. For the purposes of this book, I'll focus on the first type of trading company.

- *Manufacturers' reps.* A manufacturer's rep is someone who sells products to retailers for a manufacturer or importer. There are two kinds of manufacturers' reps, as Roger Wilson, founder and CEO of Manufacturers Representative Profile, explains:

> Some manufacturers' representatives are employee reps, or what I like to call dedicated reps, because they are dedicated to selling items from one manufacturer. They work inside the company that pays their salary, travel expenses, bonuses, and incentives and treats them like a regular employee. However, the great majority of manufacturers' representatives are independent sales reps who work on straight commission. They usually work under a master rep who owns the representative company and hires more reps who become the salespeople. The salespeople normally get two-thirds of the gross commission that the head representative collects for his or her sales. Salespeople go out, call on the account, show the product line, and pitch the lines to the buyers. If they write an order, they send it to the manufacturer. The manufacturer then ships the products to the account and pays the rep a commission. The representative group has exclusive rights to sell the accounts in that region until its contract terminates. All the accounts that the rep has obtained belong to the manufacturer or importer.

The type of manufacturers' representatives that I'll focus on here are the independent sales reps. These reps carry many lines from a variety of suppliers and usually focus on selling products from one or two types of industries in one specific geographic region.

- *Drop shipping.* As discussed in Chapter 3, drop shipping is an alternative method to buying from suppliers and taking possession of inventory. It allows you to resell and represent products that you never physically have in your possession from suppliers who handle packaging and shipping to the customer for you. This method is great for e-tailers and retailers with limited warehousing space. The retailer does not have to buy items in bulk or have warehousing capabilities. Profit is made on the difference between the price for which the reseller sells the items and the wholesale price that the retailer pays to the supplier who drop ships.

Are Trading Companies the Right Option for You?

Trading companies assist importers, wholesalers, or retailers who are sourcing from overseas for the first time. However, you need to know how to vet trading companies to avoid problems that can occur if you choose the wrong partner. Also, many people believe that working with trading companies is more expensive than working with a factory directly. I'm going to debunk this myth and also take an in-depth look at the China East Star Holding Group, a trading company located in China. Let's get to it!

When and How to Work with Trading Companies

How do you know if a trading company is right for you? You have to evaluate the services that these companies offer and decide if they're valuable to you. They can help you to manage your projects and create relationships with overseas suppliers. They have a great network and experience working with a broad range of suppliers and buyers worldwide. They also lessen language and cultural barriers because they're normally fluent in both your language and the language of the factory overseas. This is handy for both negotiating the best prices for your products and for quickly intervening should problems occur with production, quality, or logistics.

Additionally, when you're sourcing on your own, it's difficult to know which factories are credible, and you don't have the experience to assess whether the price that you're being quoted is competitive. A trading company has spent years working in the market and building strong relationships with suppliers. Its staff can help you to evaluate these types of issues. Let's look more closely at how trading companies do this.

Trading companies will assign a trade manager as your exclusive point of contact throughout the sourcing process. The trade manager will work with the factory for you and help with all logistical issues and any challenges that may occur. This can save you a lot of time when you are trying to communicate with an overseas factory. Ross McCray, founder of HomBridge, shared that he loves having a trade manager because "she deals with communication barriers and makes the whole process easier." Also, because of their market knowledge, trading companies can help to ensure that you're getting the best prices.

• • •

Trading companies are also useful for helping you to get your products manufactured correctly. When you're manufacturing a product for the first time, you usually don't know the terminology that industry professionals use. Working with people who do know the industry lingo helps to ensure that manufacturer makes the products just the way you want them.

Talia Goldfarb, cofounder of Myself Belts, explains how hiring people with industry experience can help you to avoid challenges:

> When I first started, I hired someone who worked in the retail industry to help me. She taught me how to explain what I wanted to factories. That way, when I received samples, I knew how to critique them. She also taught me about fabrics. One of the

biggest challenges in working with manufacturers overseas is explaining what you want. In China, if you say, "I want a navy canvas," there are so many different choices in navy canvases that it doesn't really mean anything to a manufacturer. That's why sending samples, and professionally explaining what you're looking for, makes the manufacturing process go faster.

Trading companies can be a quick solution to solving communication issues and getting your order right.

Trading companies also will handle purchase orders for you. Sometimes they can get you a lower MOQ than you would be able to achieve on your own. They normally represent a lot of buyers and often can consolidate all the freight they ship overseas into one order and container. This allows buyers to order lower quantities than suppliers normally require. This is so because by combining various buyers' orders in one shipment, it's cheaper for the manufacturers to send the products overseas.

• • •

Gregory Lok, CEO and cofounder of Deal Décor, explains why he recommends trading companies for small-business entrepreneurs sourcing from China:

> If you're a small business sourcing from overseas for the first time, working with a trading company can be a lot easier than working with a manufacturer. When trying to manage a manufacturer in China, there can be a lot of complications. They will forget to include an item in your container, or they'll tell you (at the last minute) that a sample isn't going to be ready when it should have been. Sometimes the issues are not major, but if you're a small company, a trading company can help manage this time-consuming process for you. Also, trading companies often push a lot of volume through manufacturers, which gives them more buying power. Trading companies can be really helpful, especially if you choose one that has been around for a while.

Finding and Vetting Trading Companies

Now that you understand how trading companies can help you, you're probably wondering how to find one. The best way to locate a trading company is by attending trade shows. Many of the big trade shows such as the ASD Trade Show, the National Hardware Show, and the MAGIC Tradeshow will have international sourcing areas. In these areas, you can find government-supported trade councils that have been brought in from each country attending the show. At MAGIC, for example, over 40 countries attend, and each brings its own trading council. These trade councils can lead you to the best and most credible trading companies. The councils are government-supported, and the trading companies they represent are usually safe options.

• • •

Another benefit of looking for a trade company at a trade show is that you can meet its trade managers. You can see whether you have chemistry with them and discover which factories they represent. Then you can research those factories at home.

A trade manager is one of the most important services that a trading company can offer you. Be sure that you're assigned one and that you get along with this person. You need to feel comfortable with him or her, and he or she needs to return e-mails and calls quickly. The trade manager also needs to be able to answer your questions precisely. He or she will become one of your biggest sources of support throughout the overseas sourcing process, so make sure that he or she gives you quality service. If he or she does, the products you source will have a higher likelihood of being exactly what you want. Having a good trade manager will make the whole process go much more smoothly. Megy Karydes, board member of the Fair Trade Federation and founder of www.World-Shoppe.com, also agrees that e-mails and communication with your overseas partners are important: "Once I had an overseas partner that only wrote me back once every three weeks. That was a sign that it was time to find someone else."

When vetting the trading companies that you come across, it's also important to make sure that they specialize in the types of products you're looking for. There are two main types of trading companies—state-owned and privately owned. Ralph Deng, CEO of China East Star Holding Group, explains the difference:

> The biggest difference between a state-owned trading company in China and a private trading company is the capital. A state-owned trading company is run and controlled by the country, while individuals control private trading companies. The export commodity structure is also different. State-owned companies are usually in control of large products like ships, trains, ammunitions, etc., and private trading companies are usually more focused on civil products like furniture, clothing, daily necessities, etc.

Find out which industries or categories the trading company you have come across has the most experience working with. Then, when you find a few that specialize in your industry, keep them on file with notes about their services. Also, get quotations from multiple trading companies and suppliers to see who will give you the best deal and service.

Potential Pitfalls of Working with Trading Companies

Although I'm an advocate for the use of trading companies, it's important to be aware of the issues that could arise when working with them. According to Renaud Anjoran's article, "Chinese Trading Companies and Their Dirty Little Secrets," from the website Quality Inspection Tips: Practical Advice to Sourcing in Asia, the three main pitfalls of working with trading companies are

1. *Some trading companies work with lower-grade factories.* Trading companies want to offer competitive prices to their customers and need to make their margins. If they don't achieve this, then buyers and suppliers frequently will cut them out and collaborate directly. So sometimes, to make their services more valuable, trading com-

panies will work with factories that don't have exporting experience. Typically, factories without experience are not well organized and have a low cost structure. And more often than not, they don't have any English speakers on staff. Often the trading company will have to do a lot of coaching to get the factory to meet the timing and quality expectations of foreign customers. This process can be very risky.

2. *Many trading companies won't tell their customers about quality issues.* Because the importers are the trading companies' customers, not the manufacturers' customers, the manufacturers often don't feel the pressure to do things exactly the way you want them. The factory knows that if it doesn't meet customers' demands, the trading company is the one that will lose money to fix the situation. Importers/buyers can ask for discounts, air shipments, or even cancel a project when things go wrong, and the trading company will cover the costs to rectify the situation with the client. Sometimes trading companies will hide serious issues from their clients to avoid frightening them.

3. *Trading companies often don't have a lot of control over the factories they work with.* Although many trading companies will act as if they own the factories, very few have actually made financial investments in them. Also, they usually work with manufacturers based on relationships rather than contracts, which can lead to insignificant or a lack altogether of penalties for poor performance.

Furthermore, Renaud's article explains that even when working with trading companies, you probably will need to take quality control into your own hands. When his clients told trading companies that they were sending their own quality agencies to test factories, the trading company would send someone first to make sure that the factories would pass quality inspection tests. However, without the clients' initiative, the trading companies wouldn't do the tests on their own.

Dominique Castro, cofounder of Twistlets, recommends sending third-party inspectors to the factories to ensure quality standards. She used SGS for inspection, verification, product testing, and certification services.

Ask for certification from factories up front, and test that products meet standards. I used SGS (sgs.com) for quality testing and inspection. This seems to be the most popular company for this service in China. They offer outsourced testing and quality control and will send people onsite to the factory if needed.

Whether you're using a trading company or working directly with the factory, use a service such as SGS to ensure the quality and safety of your products. This will force trading companies and manufacturers to take quality control more seriously.

Trading companies that don't have a financial stake in the factory have no real control over the manufacturers. The factory owner doesn't feel the pressure because he or she knows that if there are mistakes, it's the trading company that will absorb fees for canceled orders or air-freight for late shipments. Furthermore, factories often prefer working directly with foreign buyers because they believe that they have a better chance of keeping the customer.

Despite these issues, Renaud doesn't feel that all importers should source directly through manufacturers. He acknowledges the fact that there are good and bad trading companies, just as there are good and bad manufacturers. Your situation is personal, and it depends on your sourcing needs.

Renaud gave two pieces of advice for those who decide to work with trading companies:

1. *Don't trust your trading company agent with everything.* As I explained earlier, quality-control inspections are important. They are something that you need to make sure gets done, even if you have to do them yourself.
2. *Don't give all your business to one trading company.* Working with more than one trading company gives you leverage for better pricing and service.

The Truth about Price and Trading Companies

One of people's main concerns when evaluating whether or not they will work with a trading company is price. Many people overlook trading companies because they believe that working directly with the supplier is the cheapest option. However, this is not always the case. Although the price of the products may be a bit cheaper, this does not include the additional costs related to the difficulties in managing relationships with suppliers overseas. And often the added benefits offered by working with a trading company are a better choice, especially for people new to international sourcing.

Furthermore, large state-owned and privately owned trading companies often have minimal markups. Their prices are competitive to working directly with manufacturers because they often tag on a very small commission. For example, China East Star Holding Group only charges a 3 to 5 percent commission for agent services. It will be higher if the service requires more complicated work, such as quality inspection or product design, but it won't be higher than 15 percent. If the trading company is doing a good job, it actually makes a relatively small commission for the time and effort it puts in to managing the factory and solving issues that arise due to differences in language and culture. If you add up all the time that the trading company can save you from going back and forth with the factory, you could be saving thousands of dollars of your time and be protecting yourself from lost opportunities.

TIP

To get the facts about price, do your due diligence. Renaud Anjoran's article suggests that you evaluate the price quotes you receive from trading companies and make sure that they are competitive with quotes from factories. "You should spend 30 minutes asking for quotes from other suppliers of the same product before you confirm an order to a trading company. Getting an idea of the 'average market price' is quite easy." I recommend using TopTenWholesale.com and Manufacturer.com to check price quotes.

Spotlight on China East Star

Ralph Deng, CEO of the trading company China East Star Holding Group, explained a little about what makes his trading company so unique and gives advice for sourcing from overseas:

China East Star Holding Group (CES) is a large, integrated trading service company with business all over Europe, Asia, Africa, and South America. We have an annual export value of over 40,000 standard containers and have achieved success because we are different from other exporters and trading companies. We started business abroad, which makes us sharper in understanding the business requirements and habits of foreign clients. In our 16 years of business, we have trained over 300 employees to help clients find the commodities they desire through excellent communication skills, native-like English-speaking skills, and strong sourcing abilities. Furthermore, during those 16 years, we have built up an enormous supply of information in our system to ensure that we always find the right products within the shortest amount of time and at the lowest costs. And we use the most developed management software systems to guarantee the accuracy and objectivity of our work.

We feel that importers should use a trading company because China is a big country. If buyers look for the products in the Chinese market by themselves, they will get the job done but will pay a lot more than necessary and may not succeed right away. Moreover, the world is big; if factories all go abroad looking for buyers, it will lead to a similarly unsuccessful result. A trading company helps both buyers and sellers find each other successfully.

Also, since trading companies don't own factories, they aren't confined to specializing in one type of commodity; the range of products that they can help you source is much broader. If a buyer wants to source one special product, working directly with the manufacturer can be a good choice. However, if the buyer is sourcing multiple products, we recommend working with trading companies.

The best advice we can give people who want to start sourcing globally is to open their eyes widely and find a truly proficient partner. It will not only help them find the right product but also support them to grow rapidly by learning from those with extensive international trading experience. Also, to penetrate foreign markets, cut costs, and ensure company and institutional growth, concentrate your investments. You should always focus on one product or one product line and let it expand. Then reproduce the same model so that your company can grow rapidly and steadily. That way, you won't have to risk a big loss if you make the wrong investment.

Every company is in different stages of development. Don't make hurried decisions, and don't give up easily. The world is currently in an era of alliance and partnership. You can meet partners who share similar goals and reach those goals together.

Collaborating with Manufacturers' Representatives

Now let's discover the various ways to collaborate with manufacturers' representative groups. I'll explore this topic from various angles, and I'll begin by exploring the use of manufacturers' representative groups (reps) for retailers as a resource for product sourcing. Next, for those of you who want to launch your own product line and/or become an importer, I'll explain how to get reps to successfully sell your merchandise. Then I will not only teach you how to find reps but also explore the option of becoming a manufacturer's representative yourself because there is a lot of opportunity in this field.

How Manufacturers' Representatives Help Retailers

Manufacturers' rep groups are unique because most of the time you wouldn't think of them as a resource that helps retailers. They're normally associated with helping suppliers because they get their products placed in retail stores. However, I believe that they should be considered as a sourcing resource for retailers. There are manufacturers' representative groups for every industry, and you can use them to find products. If you tell the rep the type of product you're looking for, there's a good chance that he or she will know a credible factory or supplier of high quality with which to connect you.

Manufacturers' reps represent products from manufacturers, importers, exporters, and wholesalers. They work hard to know the lines they sell as well as the manufacturers themselves. Reps will help you to select the types and styles of products that you want to buy and place purchase orders for you. They will help to make choosing products and knowing what's selling well in the market easier.

They're a great resource. It's always in their best interest that the products you buy from them sell well. This raises the chances that you will buy from them again. They obviously want to sell a large amount of products from their lines because they make a commission on the items, but gaining your loyalty is just as important. And this is especially true of independent sales reps who can't afford to take on and push a product that doesn't move.

Roger Wilson, founder and CEO of Manufacturers Representative Profile, explains why independent reps are so selective:

> If a rep is good, they'll create a partnership with the retailer (aka buyer) and do everything they can to only sell them the winning lines. A reps' long-term success with a store depends on the quality of advice they give the buyer. The rep will try to show retailers the lines that do well. If a rep sells a product that ends up on the retailer's discount table, they aren't going to be working with that buyer for very long. Reps can't bury a buyer in bad merchandise. They are often even a little paranoid of selling something that

won't retail. Buyers should rely on reps to be their eyes and ears. They know what other stores are purchasing and what end customers are buying.

Megy Karydes, board member of the Fair Trade Federation and founder of www.World-Shoppe.com, explains how manufacturers' reps have been helpful for retailers like her:

Manufacturers' reps are a great resource. They've always told me what's selling in other parts of the country or what lines were doing well in my own district. And if the reps are really good, they'll take pictures of other stores' merchandising and share them with other customers. They may give you hints like, "Lucy at Peach Tree Place does this at her store in Georgia. You should consider doing it in your store in Topeka, Kansas." Reps can share a lot of helpful information that you would never otherwise receive. They can help you create a story around the product at the retail level.

Skip McGrath, online selling expert and selling coach, also shared why he likes working with reps:

I love dealing with manufacturers' reps because they know their products and are geared to giving personal service, which is what I want. I prefer to deal with a rep rather than a big manufacturing company because people at big companies change all the time, and you're not sure who you're dealing with. They have salespeople, but the salespeople tend to call on the large accounts; they don't really have time for someone like me. But the manufacturers' reps live and die with dealing with people like us, the small and medium-sized buyers.

Adam McFarlane, CEO and senior director of national accounts at manufacturers' representative agency Innovation Supplier, LLC, explains the added value that his company provides to retailers:

As manufacturers' reps, we want to understand the retailer and be a strategic partner. Being a strategic partner means bringing the retailer more than an item and a price. A manufacturer's rep should come in and say, "Here's what I see in your business. These are the gaps on your shelf. This is where you have some opportunities. This is what your competitors are doing. This is how our items are priced against our competitors. And this is how your items are priced against your competitors." At Innovation Supplier we do a complete market analysis for retailers before we even walk in the door.

• • •

Working with manufacturers' reps can provide many added benefits to retailers and can help you to find products that will sell. Jason Hoffman, senior manager of global brand merchandising in the Entertainment Division of Walmart, explained how manufacturers' reps help the world's largest retailer. "They are one of the many partners that help us to stay connected to the best business network possible. They are a quality source that allows us to track each component of a product to the source of origin, which is imperative."

It's additionally important to note that if you meet a rep who doesn't work in your territory but has products you like or you simply prefer working directly with suppliers, there are situations where manufacturers' reps will connect you directly with suppliers. Sometimes they have an agreement worked out with suppliers in advance to receive a percentage if they connect you with them. Reps can only work with a finite number of buyers and factories at a time. Sometimes it's to their benefit that you order directly from the manufacturer. You won't get the additional help, but this could be a good tactic if you're looking to source one unique product from a manufacturer.

Manufacturers' Reps for Suppliers

If you're going to become a supplier yourself by manufacturing products, importing goods, or selling mass amounts of wholesale items, you need to open up sales channels and get your products into the market. You can spend money on marketing and advertising and exhibiting at trade shows (these are great tactics), but for some new suppliers these tactics are too expensive when just starting out. Another less expensive way to get products into the market is by having manufacturers' reps represent your line. Many rep groups can represent your line both nationally and internationally. This can be an easy way to get your products in front of really big buyers with whom these reps have already developed relationships.

Ed Juline, a partner at the manufacturers' representative company Mexico Representation, explains the difference between market-entry strategies for large and small companies. He also explains why a manufacturer's representative is helpful for small to medium-sized companies that want to get their products into retail stores:

Big companies have different strategies than small companies when entering a market for the first time. They're already established and usually looking to conquer markets one by one. They will hire country managers and four or five salespeople for each region. They usually have a lot of money to invest, so they will also set up new warehouses and local distribution methods.

When you're a smaller company, you don't want this kind of overhead and need a different approach. You'll want to find a representative or an agent and advertise online. A manufacturer's rep agency is good for small to medium-sized businesses because they become an extension of your sales force. And they provide the local touch and support that you need when you're trying to enter a new market. People want to do business with people they know and like. Even with the global economy and technology we have today, long-distance sales are still hard without someone in the country helping you.

Rep groups are the most cost-effective way to distribute your product because they already have an established network. Also, you don't have to pay them a salary, benefits, and other fees related to employees. All you have to do is give them a commission, and they will open up sales funnels for you.

Ed further explains the lack of risk to companies when working with manufacturers' reps: "There is less risk to the company because you're not paying that salary every month. The company benefits because they only have to pay for what gets sold." This is much more practical for new companies just starting out and for long-standing small to medium-sized companies that don't want to maintain the extra overhead.

When a good rep group decides to represent your products, you'll be provided with many more sales opportunities. You'll have a sales team all across the country (or various countries) that can meet face to face with small to medium-sized retailers and big-box retail chain buyers. They'll expand your customer base with relationships established through selling other manufacturers' products. If they're good, they'll have a great network.

Advice for Getting Reps to Sell Your Product Line

Now that you understand how a manufacturer's rep agency can help your business, let's discuss how to get them to represent your line. A manufacturer's rep is going to look for a winning product line. The rep needs to be sure that the line will sell well and that there's a need for your product in the market. You have to prove that when your product hits the stores, it will show a fast increase in sales for the rep. You have to build a case and go prepared.

TIP

When you pitch your line to a manufacturers' representative group, go with a presentation that demonstrates why they should want to represent your products. You're asking them to sell your products to buyers with whom they need to maintain strong relationships. It's important to convince them of the benefits of your products.

Roger Wilson gave me some tips on how you can motivate a rep to take on your line:

We suggest that suppliers call the top four rep picks in each territory. They should use the first phone call to let the rep know that they're exploring various options to set up a competitive element from the start. However, it's important that you don't reveal who the competition is because you can use their curiosity against them. Every rep has other rep agencies that are competing for the same lines and that sell to the same customers in their territory. A rep is the ultimate competitor. Every time he goes in front of a buyer, he is competing; he wins when he gets an order, and he loses when he doesn't.

As a manufacturer or supplier, you can use this to your advantage by explaining that you've had quite a few reps interested in carrying your line. Explain that you have eight or ten options but that the rep on the phone is one of the first people you have called. This creates a perceived value of your product line. And if the rep does end up representing your line, they'll already have an incentive to succeed. They won't want to lose the line to another rep.

Another way to motivate and get good performance from a rep is by providing him or her with the proper preparation materials. Roger explained that before pitching your line to a representative, you should take into account how he or she makes a living. Reps are independent contractors and make their own choices. They're not like a regular employee whose salary you pay. Independent contractors choose what they want to go out and sell every day. You need to show them that taking the time to sell your line will be worth their time. There are things you can do to tailor your program to the way reps work. You want to make it easier for them to achieve success.

• • •

Roger Wilson shared that when pitching your line to a rep, it's important to provide the rep with the right materials so that he or she feels motivated to sell your products:

> If a rep appears interested in your line, send them information right away. At Manufacturers Representative Profile we suggest sending the rep these five things after the first phone call:
>
> 1. *An eight-and-a-half-by-eleven single-sheet color catalogue.* I recommend single-sheet catalogues because when the rep shows the line to the buyer, they can do it in specific segments. They can pitch the retailer one product at a time so that they're able to see the full spectrum and benefits of each product. If the rep hands the buyer a bound catalogue, they may flip through it quickly and think that they are not interested in the line. When a rep uses single sheets, they have a better chance of working the line with the buyer. They can take the time to go through the good-selling items as well as the best sizes, colors, styles, and more with the buyer.
> 2. *A price sheet.* The price sheet should have space so that the rep can easily and conveniently convert it into an order form when working with buyers.
> 3. *Audio cassette or CD with the selling points of your items.* A lot of reps spend a significant amount of time in their car driving to see buyers. This is a great chance to get their attention and teach them the important points about your line. The CD should be the sales pitch, or what I call the "golden words." It's essentially what the rep will tell the buyer to sell your line.
> 4. *Product samples.* By sending these, the rep can show buyers a real-life example of the product on the catalogue sheet.
> 5. *Policies and procedures.* This helps lay out your terms and conditions so that the rep knows how you do business. It should include your terms of sales, your minimum orders, and other important information about your company's procedures.

TIP

Not only do you need to provide the rep with your products' benefits but you also should include points that will cancel out any objections that buyers may have to purchasing the merchandise. When a rep shows a line, there are often certain doubts that buyers will have. The best thing for the rep to do is cancel those out in the beginning. The buyer may not bring up the objections, but often he or she is thinking them. Doing market research will help you to know what those types of objections are.

By sending this information you show the rep that you are organized and serious about your business. The rep will be more interested in working with you because he or she can feel confident that you will set him or her up for success. This is important because the easier it is for the rep to understand your company's products, the easier it will be for him or her to pitch and sell them to buyers.

Adam McFarlane also explained some of the things he looks for when choosing whether or not to represent a line:

I have relationships with some of the top buyers in the country, including Walmart, Target, Costco, Sam's Club, and more. A lot of manufacturers and importers want to get their lines into these stores, and I get e-mails from them daily saying, "Hey, I have a great product. What do you think?" I find that many companies want to run before they walk. They think, "Hey, this would be great at Walmart," but it's a bit more complicated than just having a great product. If you get into a store like Walmart, you will sell over half a million units a year, and sometimes many more. It's a huge amount of work to get your logistics set up to be able to meet this type of demand. Suppliers need to make sure that they have the capabilities to handle a large account.

Before I even look into this market to see if their products fit, I ask the suppliers the following questions:

1. Do you have the logistics to be in the store you are interested in entering?
2. Are your finances in order?
3. Do you have a Dun & Bradstreet number and a good rating?
4. Do you have electronic data interchange (EDI) capabilities?
5. Do you have the necessary insurance?
6. What are the retailer's opportunities in taking on your line?
7. In what type and size of store does your item belong?
8. How do your products compare with items that are already in the types of stores that you would like to sell to?
9. What differentiates your product besides cost?

If a manufacturer wants to use our company, we need to know why it makes sense to rep their line.

TIP

Adam McFarlane also explained that if you're a small business and interested in getting your products into one of the big retail chains, you should start by selling your products to an already established distributor that has a supplier contract with the retail chain. That way, the distributor can sell your products to mass merchants for you. This is a good tactic because generally you shouldn't sell to a big-box retailer if they will make up more than 20 percent of your portfolio. Most big chains won't even take on your line because they don't want to be responsible for putting you out of business if they decide to stop carrying your product. Work your way up through smaller stores and distributors first, and then go into the big chains once you're established.

GETTING YOUR PRODUCTS INTO WALMART

I asked Jason Hoffman, senior manager of global brand merchandising in the Entertainment Division of Walmart, how the biggest retailer in the world vets suppliers, and what you can do to get your products into their stores. Here's what he explained:

The supplier vetting process differs in each division at Walmart. Some of the core prerequisites are based on the supplier's capabilities and their execution history. Finding the right partnership starts with the supplier's ability to meet the needs of our team, followed by a good initial face-to-face meeting and excellent references. Once these steps are completed, the next steps vary based on the timing of the necessary deliverables.

The question to ask yourself when thinking of entering our marketplace is, "What makes this product different than what already exists, and what makes people want to buy this product over similar items?" If you can answer these questions in detail before you set up the meeting, you are starting out on the right foot.

You need to be the expert. Once you feel like you know your product inside and out, evaluate the competitive marketplace. Are there products that already exist in the marketplace that fulfill the same needs or purpose as your product(s)? How does your product compare in tangible aspects, user friendliness, features, size, and more to those products? If you prepare for the meeting as "The Expert," and share your knowledge by showcasing that you know the business, your opinion will be respected. This is in line with our core values and the value of "Respect for the Individual."

Also, be prepared to answer follow-up questions on the spot. If you don't know the answers to those questions, propose that you will get back to us with the answers in the next 24 hours. Know your product inside and out, as well as the insights, trends, and future projections for its ability to perform in the marketplace. Be ready to be challenged, and you will be headed down the path to success.

Being an expert about your products is imperative for your success. Adam McFarlane also added that although manufacturers' reps can help you to become more knowledgeable about the marketplace (and about creating relationships that lead to sales opportunities), it's important to stay involved and remember that it's still *your* company:

> When you are choosing a manufacturer's rep, understand that no one cares for your business more than you do. A lot of times manufacturers will hand over their products and think, "It's not my business anymore." Well, it is your business; it's your livelihood, so be extremely involved with your reps or distributors. Set them up for success. Make sure that they have the information they need. Explain the opportunities that your products will create for retailers and help do the market analysis. Put your reps in the best position to win.

Where to Find Manufacturers' Representative Groups

Now that you understand how important and helpful reps are, you're probably wondering where to find them. A lot of times the best way to find a manufacturer's rep is at trade shows. There are directories that will explain where manufacturers' reps are located on the show floor. This is a good way to find reps because if they are in the directory, you know that they're credible and approved by the trade-show staff.

Another way to find rep groups is through the Internet. You can always do a regular search for terms such as "manufacturers' rep," "sales agents," "mfg rep," or "manufacturer's representative." I also highly recommend using vertical search engines that cater to finding reps. They have unique profiling systems that help you to find the right rep groups based on your needs.

Some of the best vertical search engines that target reps include

- GreatRep.com. This is an Internet directory for reps in the wholesale giftware, home furnishing, and furniture industries.
- ManaOnline.org. The Manufacturers' Agents National Association has many resources for both reps and manufacturers who are

getting started in this business. They also have RepFinder on their site, which is a database that has reps from various industries.

- MRPusa.com. Manufacturers Representative Profile's database covers all types of consumer-product representatives and also offers consulting services on how to work with reps.
- RepHunter.net. This is a rep database that targets its search to various industries and territories. It helps to match manufacturers and distributors with independent sales representatives.
- RepLocate.com. Because it is under the parent company RepHunter .net, RepLocate.com has a database with a similar function. It helps to connect manufacturers with manufacturers' representatives, and it covers a wide variety of industries.

These sites are extremely helpful in connecting suppliers and manufacturers. They've been in the industry a long time and have proven to help people find manufacturers' reps. On RepHunter.net's website you can read testimonials from many people who have shared their success stories about these services. Following is one example of a testimonial featured on the RepHunter.net website from Melissa Wright, owner of Bamboo Bebe: "This is a wonderful website/service, and I will certainly pass the link along to anyone I think could benefit from it. We have made contact with several reps and have had much success. What a wonderful service!" Also, if you want to vet any of these rep-locating companies in person, you often can find them at trade shows as well.

ARE YOU INTERESTED IN BECOMING A REP?

Becoming a rep could be a great way to build relationships and make some extra cash on the side as you are developing a product line. It's a great way to get to know the industry and meet a lot of important industry players as your business grows. You network with tons of people and meet lots of buyers. And who knows, perhaps you could make a connection with a retail chain that eventually might have the need for the type of product line you would like to develop.

(continued)

• • •

Ed Juline explains some of the benefits of being a manufacturer's rep and some of the keys to becoming a successful rep:

> Being a manufacturer's rep is different than being a salesperson for a company. Apart from the fun of being an entrepreneur, there are many benefits associated with representing multiple companies. One of the keys to becoming a successful rep is measuring your work versus revenue. Most people get paid for the hours of work they do at their job. When you are a rep or an agent, it's not measured like that. You get paid for value. If you can make the right connection and close a deal in an hour, and that deal is worth a million dollars, then you just made a percentage of a million dollars an hour. However, if it takes you three months to close a deal and all you make is a thousand dollars, your time doesn't measure correctly with your compensation. That's one of the big metrics that new reps don't measure well. You need to think about how much money you're going to make for the amount of effort you put in.

Ed also explains the importance of time management and warns that if you really want to go into this industry as your full-time career, you need to be prepared:

> Being an independent rep is a form of guerrilla warfare. You really need to be a survivor. It's different from working for a salary, where you get paid whether you sell or not. When you are an independent contractor, you can' t have many bad days. You've got to schedule your time right and be good at managing it. It's not easy to be talented at this and make a good living. The reps that are good make a lot of money, but you have to have skills. No one guarantees you anything; you have to go out and make it happen.

Ed explained that if you're interested in this profession, you should go to the buying marts or trade shows and find an established sales rep company to work for. Working with such a company allows you to get to know the business and the buyers with whom it already has connections. In addition, you will have a base income from the company's already established accounts as you are making new connections. Ed believes that it usually takes about a year and a half before you really start making a good income. Also, if this is an opportunity that you'd like to pursue, the platforms that I listed in the "Where to Find Manufacturers' Representative Groups" section earlier in this chapter are great resources to help get you started.

Understanding the Pros, Cons, and Various Types of Drop Shipping

You're already familiar with what drop shipping is from Chapter 3. You know that it's helpful for retailers who don't have a lot of warehouse space or who can't buy large quantities of products at a time. But how do you know whether this is the right approach for your company? Let's examine the pros and cons of using this method and explore the types of drop-shipping companies available.

The Pros of Drop Shipping

Drop shipping has many benefits for small to medium-sized retailers. Brandon Delgrosso, president and CEO of Doba (a web-based inventory-on-demand platform that helps retailers connect with suppliers that drop ship), shared some of the benefits associated with drop shipping:

1. Drop shipping lowers the risk of starting or growing an online retail business by not tying up capital in product inventory and warehouse space.

2. Suppliers take care of the warehousing, packaging, and shipping of the products, which saves you a great deal of money.
3. Drop shipping allows the retailer to conduct product market research with very little investment and risk. The retailer can test new brands and product variations to understand demand and shelf life before buying in bulk. It can be used as a discovery tool for retailers.
4. The retailer pays for products only after they are sold and they receive payment from their customers.
5. Drop shipping allows retailers to focus more time and resources on other activities such as marketing, advertising, product research, and more.

Brandon also explained some reasons to use drop shipping and the situations in which it best functions:

The decision to drop ship in lieu of importing and inventorying comes down to three factors: risk, capital (cash), and growth. Drop shipping reduces risk, as capital is not tied up in inventory and warehouses. It also allows the retailer to sell more product types and attributes because they have an unlimited amount of virtual shelf space.

Additionally, drop shipping helps retailers have a diverse product sourcing strategy. Retailers should import and inventory their best-selling products (with short shelf life), allowing inventory to rotate more frequently in their warehouses. And they should drop ship products that tend to have a longer shelf life, which can potentially tie up valuable space in their warehouses.

For example, black and white blenders are the hottest selling colors for home appliances. However, there are people who will want camouflage blenders. As a retailer with limited storage space, you don't want to tie up your storage space with camouflage blenders. But you do want to fulfill your customers' needs. The solution here is to drop ship the camouflage blender and create a wining situation for all parties involved.

Jay Cheng, CEO and cofounder of J Goodin Inc., drop ships products for his customers and confirms that retailers need to have a stable inventory base and be selective when choosing the products they drop ship:

> I recommend drop shipping for someone who already has an inventory-based business of their own and uses drop shipping as an accessory to their core business in specific product groups. As a retailer, you need to have a core group of products that you own and distribute. You should own the products that provide you with your regular income because that's how you will have the highest gross margin in the products. You are able to buy goods for less when you buy a higher quantity and stock them yourself. You also have more control in getting products to your customers when you want them to get there.

Skip McGrath, online selling expert and online selling coach, is a big fan of drop shipping and a great example of someone who makes money using this method:

> I love drop shipping; we drop ship half of our products. I'm a big fan because it's very profitable. However, I prefer to work with manufacturers and distributors that keep the products they drop ship in their own warehouses. That way, they can provide me with better customer service when I need it. There are a lot of suppliers that drop ship this way, and a lot of them advertise on TopTenWholesale.

The Cons of Drop Shipping

Now let's look at some of the issues that come into play when working with suppliers that drop ship. Brandon Delgrosso explained why he always recommends that retailers have a well-balanced product-sourcing and fulfillment strategy:

> One of the downsides to drop shipping is profit margin. Because the supplier is continuing to warehouse, package, and ship the

products for the retailer, they are not able to offer bulk pricing on the products. This is where importing and inventorying have a huge advantage. If you have the capital, warehousing, and logistics, then importing and inventorying your own products can yield a high profit margin. The strategy for the retailer is to decide which products make sense to import and inventory versus drop ship.

Brandon also explained some drawbacks to drop shipping:

1. You lose some control over shipping times, packaging processes, and packaging branding. However, with more suppliers embracing drop shopping for online retailers, they are making strides such as expedited shipping and branded package slips.
2. Your supplier may run out of hot-selling products.
3. Extra drop-ship fees are charged for handling per shipped order. This can reduce your profit margins.
4. You have lower profit margins than if you were to buy the products in bulk. However, the higher profit margins associated with buying in bulk can be eaten up by warehousing, packaging, and personnel costs. It's important to take those additional costs into consideration when calculating the true profit margin per product.

Jay Cheng confirmed that you have to be smart when drop shipping. He explains that when choosing this method, retailers can't expect that the products will always be available to their customers:

The bad thing about drop shipping is that from time to time things run out of stock. If something is a hot seller for the retailer and a hot seller for the supplier, the supplier is going to have to sell that item to their customers first. You give up control for saving costs and having more cash flow. However, drop shipping is a really efficient model if done correctly.

Third-Party Drop Shipping Companies

There are two kinds of drop shippers—regular manufacturers/whole-salers who have drop-shipping programs and third-party drop shippers who work with anywhere from ten to hundreds of manufacturers. Third-party drop shippers buy a certain amount of products from manufacturers and wholesalers a year and handle the delivery of the items to your customers.

Brandon Delgrosso explains what his company, Doba, does as a third-party drop shipper:

> Doba is the industry-leading distributor of products for online retail entrepreneurs and small business. It simplifies drop shipping by providing instant access to millions of products that can be drop shipped directly to customers. Our tools aggregate product data such as product images, descriptions, inventory updates, wholesale pricing, and shipping from hundreds of suppliers, distributors, and manufactures.
>
> We pride ourselves as being the one-stop shop for both online retailers and suppliers. With only one Doba account, an entrepreneur can have instant access to hundreds of suppliers, thousands of brands, and millions of products. In addition, with only one account, suppliers gain access to a rich base of online retailers looking for products to sell. We are the perfect two-sided marketplace for retailers and suppliers. We aggregate orders from thousands of retailers, which gives us an increased buying power with suppliers. We are able to get the lowest drop-shipping prices for our network of suppliers, and we pass these savings and negotiated rates on to our retailer base.

There are many drop-shipping companies that function in a similar fashion as Doba. Some of the third-party drop-shipping companies that I recommend include

- *Doba:* www.doba.com/
- *Kole Imports:* http://koleimports.com/

- *Worldwide Brands:* www.worldwidebrands.com/
- *Via Trading Corporation:* www.viatrading.com/
- *Sunrise Wholesale Merchandise:* http://sunrisewholesalemerchandise.com/
- *Gift Basket Drop Shipping:* www.giftbasketdropshipping.com/
- *Innex, Inc.:* www.innexinc.com/
- *HandbagsWholesale.com:* http://handbagswholesale.com/

All these companies are a great solution for finding a myriad of factories and suppliers that drop ship.

Conclusion

Throughout this chapter you have learned about many important services that can help you to source products more easily. You better understand why and how to work with trading companies and the importance of being assigned a trade manager. You're also familiar with manufacturers' reps and how they can be a great resource for your company whether you're a retailer or a supplier. Additionally, you learned how to set them up for success, how to get into big-box retail chains, and how to break into the manufacturer rep business. Furthermore, you know the pros and cons of working with suppliers that drop ship and are familiar with some of the companies that can help you drop ship from multiple suppliers. I hope that I have opened your eyes to new sourcing solutions and that you understand more about who can help you source (and sell) products.

Looking Ahead

In Chapter 7, you'll learn about the importance of building and maintaining strong relationships with your new sourcing partners. I'll discuss not only the ways to select strong partners but also how to professionally cultivate and foster these relationships. You'll have the keys to maintaining healthy relationships and know the signs that tell you when it's time to move on. I'll also teach you how to manage relationships with your suppliers. This is one of the most important components to running a successful retail or wholesale business. When you learn how to do it correctly, it yields profit and satisfied customers.

7

Better Supply-Chain Management through Building and Nurturing Strong Relationships with Suppliers

The key elements in the art of working together are how to deal with change, how to deal with conflict, and how to reach our potential. . . . the needs of the team are best met when we meet the needs of individual persons.

—*Max De Pree (1924–), author and former CEO of Herman Miller, Inc.*

IN CHAPTER 6, you learned how to work with trading companies, manufacturers' reps, and suppliers that drop ship. You now understand how each of these partners can help you with different sourcing necessities. I also touched on the importance of choosing the right sourcing partners because they can help to make your business run more smoothly and successfully.

In this chapter, I'll further discuss how to build and nurture relationships with your trading partners. Not only will you learn how to foster those relationships, but you'll also learn how closely linked and important they are for evaluating and managing your supply chain. Building and nurturing strong relationships involves more than just choosing partners that you get along with; it's about making good business decisions and running your supply chain successfully.

When most people hear the term *supply chain*, they automatically start thinking about the end product and the manufacturers, exporters, wholesalers, and producers that help them to obtain that product. However, there's much more involved. Your supply chain is the heartbeat of your business. It's what keeps it running and functioning properly. The Council of Supply Chain Management Professionals (CSCMP) defines *supply-chain management* as follows:

> Supply Chain Management encompasses the planning and management of all activities involved in sourcing and procurement, conversion, and all logistics management activities. Importantly, it also includes coordination and collaboration with channel partners, which can be suppliers, intermediaries, third-party service providers, and customers. In essence, Supply Chain Management integrates supply and demand management within and across companies. Supply Chain Management is an integrating function with primary responsibility for linking major business functions and business processes within and across companies into a cohesive and high-performing business model. It includes all of the logistics management activities noted above, as well as manufacturing operations. It drives coordination of processes and activities with and across marketing, sales, product design, finance, and information technology.

Essentially, every part of your retail or wholesale business makes up your supply chain. I urge you to keep your supply chain updated by designing a diagram. It can show all the players involved in your business: the company that makes the raw materials, the manufacturing company, the supplier (if different from the manufacturer), the methods of distribution, your business, the go-to-market strategy, the points of sale, and the consumer. By creating a chart with this information, you can see all the players involved and keep them in order. It provides you with a quick snapshot of your operations, and they are mapped out clearly. Now I will provide you with critical steps to managing your supply chain and share tips about how to govern relationships with your trading partners.

Managing Your Supply Chain Effectively

How you manage your supply chain will determine whether your business succeeds or fails. It's that important. Keeping the supply chain under control is essential because many problems can occur when it's not structured properly. For example, many new entrepreneurs will start working with a supplier and feel really enthusiastic about the product they're sourcing. They will develop a go-to-market strategy, create their product with the help of multiple suppliers, and attend trade shows as a vendor. Perhaps they will even meet with big retailers that are interested in their products. And then, all of a sudden, when they're finally getting the attention of big buyers, they'll hear objections about their product's prices being too high. The buyer may even explain that he or she knows some people with similar items at a much lower price.

Ross McCray, cofounder of HomBridge, explains when he realized that he could be getting better pricing and using more effective partners:

> My partner and I didn't have any experience sourcing products; this was our first time. We went online and did a Google search for companies that manufacture silicone and rubber. We received price quotes and found a supplier who we thought had pretty good prices. We started working with this factory and believed that our margins were really good until we met with Jason, who explained that we could improve our profit margins and receive better service from our suppliers. He helped us and made both of these promises come true.
>
> Changing to a different sourcing partner opened up a lot of doors. It gives us a stronger financial position for marketing and the ability to offer better prices to our customers. And, in addition to getting a better price, we also get better service. Now we work

with a trade manager who handles the communication with the factory for us. These two elements have made a huge difference, and now we can do a lot more with our product.

Luckily, Ross was still in the early stages of developing his product. He hadn't sold it to the big chains yet, and he was able to get help from an expert early on. If he hadn't made these changes, though, he may have run into problems finding buyers that were willing to pay the prices for which he was offering his products. He would have been in the familiar (for many people) and unfortunate position of having a great product with bad pricing. Having had no experience in global trade, he would have stuck with the original supplier, taken his product to stores, and at the last moment, after having spent a ton of money, realized that he desperately needed to find a new supplier. If you find that your prices are too high for your customers, regardless of whether you're launching a new product line or buying products wholesale, you need to go back to your supply chain and reevaluate where you can cut costs.

The Importance of Choosing the Right Partners from the Start

Where and how you find your suppliers are usually good indicators of whether or not they'll be good partners for you and whether they'll keep your supply-chain costs down. When you are evaluating suppliers, you need to consider where your supplier should be located. You need to choose someone regionally, domestically, or internationally. Remember, being able to see your partner face to face (or have someone do this for you) is going to be an important aspect of managing and developing your supply chain and the relationship. Nikhil Jain, CEO of OnGreen, suggests "spend[ing] some time at their offices and talk[ing] not only with the executive team but also with the middle- and lower-level people." This helps to ensure that the supplier is credible and that you are getting the best price and service from that supplier. Choosing a credible partner sets a foundation and allows your supply chain to function more properly. You need to constantly evaluate your relationship with suppliers through rating systems and measurement tools, which I will discuss later on in this chapter. For now, it's important to know that the success of your product is going to depend on the supplier from whom you're sourcing.

Mike Bellamy, owner of PassageMaker Sourcing Solutions, agrees that working with the right supplier is the most important element in the supply chain:

> If you have issued a purchase order to a bad supplier because you failed to verify them, unfortunately, no amount of even the world's best project management or intense quality control is going to be able to make a bad supplier great. If, however, you find a good supplier early on, you have put yourself on the right path, and both project management and quality control will be much easier.

Here are some of Mike's tips for choosing the right partners overseas. However, these can be applied to choosing domestic suppliers as well.

1. Pick a factory that is the right size for your order. If you are a small buyer at a large factory, you will find it hard to keep their attention.
2. Make sure that you communicate with the suppliers on a regular basis. If you aren't asking for updates, you are unlikely to receive them. Be in contact when there is good news to share so that you don't become the "headache client" who contacts the factory only when things are bad.
3. This may sound obvious, but if you and your supplier don't have a system for project management, then you need to be proactive and create one. For example, a simple Excel spreadsheet listing action items, project dates, deadlines, and responsible parties is a huge improvement over trying to manage via e-mail. Have this open-project list serve as the agenda for periodic conference calls with your supplier. Once

the tasks are mutually agreed on, save this document for future reference. Keep a record of each week's agreed steps.

4. Build into your budget the costs of a few international trips to the factory to keep an eye on things and build a good working relationship with your supplier. If you can't afford to travel on your own or don't want to make the trip, get an agent to represent you.

5. If you only take away one of these tips, I hope you remember the following: Link payments to performance. You are crazy to make the final payment to a supplier without inspecting the goods first with your own eyes and then with the eyes of a third party that works for you.

How to Choose Reliable and Strong Suppliers over "Price Is Right" Suppliers

Before choosing a supplier, you should ask about the payment terms and how the supplier accepts your money. Find out if the supplier accepts escrow, letters of credit, cash, money orders, credit cards, Alipay, or Pay-Pal. This can tell you a lot about the company's trustworthiness. If the company only accepts cash, you should be weary of working with it. All companies in China must have a certain amount of registered capital. For example, when doing business with an exporter in China, ask the representative for a statement that proves how much capital the company has registered. Never work with a Chinese supplier who has no liquidity or a poor Dun & Bradstreet rating.

Before working with a supplier, ask if the supplier's customers have been reordering and/or if the supplier is developing new products. Ask what the supplier's plans for growth are in the next year. Be sure you also know the supplier's plans for product development. Ask what new products are in the pipeline and how you can get in early on distribution. You have the right to know, and it never hurts to do this type of due diligence.

However, keep in mind that asking about payment terms and how business is going is very different from focusing on the price of the products. Choosing a supplier is not all about price! If people only bought items based on price, they would limit themselves to buying low-quality merchandise from wishy-washy suppliers. Communication, reliability, and quality are equal to comfort and security. Price is important, but do a thorough evaluation to see what you're paying for. For example, it's worth the extra money if you're paying for higher-quality products. Your customers will care about quality and be willing to pay a little more for that value.

But don't be fooled into overpaying either. Michael Fan, CEO and general manager of New Times, explains that if a price is too low or too high, you should be wary of that supplier's services:

> You can always identify a real exporter by verifying if their price quotation is within the normal price range. You don't want a supplier who offers you a quote much higher or much lower than this amount. Additionally, an experienced exporter should know the competitors in your market well. They should know the various brands as well as the advantages and disadvantages about the nuances of various products. Also, an experienced exporter should be familiar with all kinds of certification, such as VDE, GS, FCC, CSA, EMC, TUV, and ROHS [for definitions of these certifications, see Table 7-1] and always be ready to discuss which certification a buyer needs and which they should apply for from third-party vendors.

TIP

To know if a supplier's prices are in the right range, do your due diligence about market prices, or speak with someone at TopTenWholesale.com or Manufacturer.com.

Table 7-1 Product Certification Terms

Your manufacturer should know which certifications your products need, but here is a list of some that may be relevant for your business (depending on where you would like to see your products). There are different tests for selling to different markets. Knowing these certifications can help you to do due diligence on your suppliers. Ask if your suppliers know about the following tests:

VDE: German Electrical Engineers Association	Tests: Lighting equipment, electronic equipment, information technology (IT) products, wire and cable, industrial and medical electrical equipment, household electrical appliances, business equipment and systems, electronic and electrical components, materials testing, and environmental testing
GS (Germany Safety)	Tests: Household appliances such as washing machines, refrigerators, and kitchen appliances; household machines; sporting goods; home electronics devices such as audiovisual equipment; electrical and electronic office equipment such as fax machines, copiers, shredders, printers, and computers; industrial machinery; laboratory measuring equipment; and security-related products such as helmets, furniture, ladders, and bicycles
FCC (Federal Communications Commission)	Tests: All types of manufactured and imported goods.
CSA (Canadian Standards Association)	Tests: Building materials, machinery, office equipment, computer equipment, electrical appliances, environmental protection, sports and entertainment, health care, fire safety, and all types of security products
EMC (European Common Market)	Tests: Multiple moving motor vehicles such as trucks, buses, passenger cars, and motorcycles; lamps and light bulbs; mirrors, tires, wheels, brakes, horns, antitheft devices, seat belts, exhaust pipes, and automotive glass;

	and vehicle accessories such as car seats, helmets, and car electrical products
TUV (Technical Inspection Association)	Tests: A wide range of industries worldwide, including consumer products; retail; textile, clothing, and footwear; furniture/office equipment; and much more (Go to www.tuvamerica.com/ for a full list of industries for which it provides certifications.)
ROHS (Restriction of Hazardous Substances Directive)	Tests: IT and telecommunications equipment; small household appliances; large household appliances; consumer equipment; electronic and electrical tools; toys, leisure, and sports equipment; light bulbs and lighting equipment; automatic dispensers; and semiconductor devices

In addition to the FCC certification, some of the other most common certifications for selling products in the United States include

UL (Underwriters Laboratories)	Tests: Product and operational safety
ASTM. ASTM International, formerly known as the American Society for Testing and Materials (ASTM)	Tests: Range from metals to construction materials and petroleum to consumer products
FDA (U.S. Food and Drug Administration)	Tests: Food, drugs, cosmetics, biologic products, medical devices, veterinary drugs, and diagnostic supplies management
EPA (U.S. Environmental Protection Agency)	Tests: A broad range of products and businesses
Energy Star. A requirement for the U.S. Department of Energy and the EPA	Tests: Household products
ETL (Electrical Testing Laboratories)	Tests: Product operated with electricity

For more information about these certifications, and to find out which could apply to your businesses' products, go to /www.wstlab.com/

Ed Juline, founder of Mexico Representation, also explains that choosing a supplier has to do with the value the supplier provides to you:

A lot of people make the big mistake of focusing solely on price. Choosing a supplier is about so much more than price. You've got to look at the total cost and the value they provide you. Let's say I get quotes from three Chinese suppliers. One can make my product for one dollar a unit, another for two dollars, and the third for three dollars. The dollar supplier answers e-mails three days late. The three-dollar supplier is from a world-class European organization that has a factory in China. The two-dollar supplier is from a reliable company that has a good website and English speakers who answer the phone when you call. Depending on your needs, the two-dollar supplier could be the best one to choose. It's a combination of price, service, and quality. If you just focus on the bottom-line price and don't take all the other factors into account, you will eventually lose. The importance of looking at these factors is the same no matter where in the world you are hiring your suppliers. You can't be focused completely on price.

There are so many other benefits that a supplier can provide that are more important than getting a low price. Don't count your pennies when it comes to choosing a supplier, or you may end up being sorry later. Instead, focus on the stability and reliability of potential suppliers. "Be HIP," and choose suppliers that are HIP.

What do I mean by HIP? This is TopTenWholesale.com and Manufacturer.com's internal company policy. HIP means "*h*onesty, *i*ntegrity, and *p*rofessionalism." It's something I learned when I was finishing up my law administration degree, and it has been a cornerstone and pillar that drives success in my business. I may at times seem rough around the edges, but you can't knock me for my integrity, credibility, and who I am as a person. TopTenWholesale.com and Manufacturer.com are HIP companies.

Establishing Key Performance Indicators and Benchmarks

One way to evaluate the company you're working with (or are thinking about working with) is by establishing some good performance indicators. At TopTenWholesale.com and Manufactur.com, we work off of key performance indicators (KPIs) and benchmarks. Although originally created to measure internal performance, I suggest using them to vet and evaluate suppliers. For our purposes, KPIs are values and goals that help you to evaluate the performance of your supplier's business, and benchmarking is the act of comparing your supplier's performance with that of other stand-out suppliers in the industry. These measurement tools help you to ensure that suppliers are working according to your standards and goals.

An example of the type of performance that you can evaluate with KPIs and benchmarks is timeliness of e-mails. If someone only gets back to you once every three days or even less often, this suggests that he or she is not a good person to work with. A KPI could be "responds to e-mails within 24 hours or less" (depending on where the supplier is located).

This may sound simple, but Dominique Castro, cofounder of Twistlets, explains that when working with partners overseas, things seemingly simple such as responding to e-mails quickly become very important:

Don't deal with someone who doesn't respond quickly. And make sure that they respond accurately. Did they send you a generic response that they send to all inquires, or was their e-mail response personal and tailored to your needs?

It's important to be aware of and look for these types of signals from the beginning.

David Stankunas, founder of Beard Head, also adds that in addition to quick communication, *courteous* communication should be a benchmark not only for your suppliers but also for you and your team as well:

> I expect a quick response whenever I ask a question, and I respond quickly to my suppliers' questions as well. Even a simple "Yes" helps your partners realize that you received the information and helps you gain respect. Sometimes Americans can be curt. I don't communicate that way with my overseas manufacturers because they don't communicate that way with me. Starting with a gracious introduction helps build the relationship and show the supplier that you care. Ask your partner how things are going, and you will see better results in the long term.

Besides communication in e-mails, there are many other benchmarks and KPIs that you will want to take into account when evaluating your suppliers. Here is a list of some benchmark criteria that you can use to assess your partners:

1. Product output capacity
2. Financial stability
3. Quality assurance
4. Organizational structure
5. Manufacturing or delivery processes
6. Performance

You can evaluate each of these areas individually and tailor them to what you are looking for in a supplier. Setting up standards from the start helps you to make good business decisions and know whether you're working with the right supplier.

Specific Criteria for Formally Evaluating Suppliers

If you want to evaluate suppliers in a formal manner (which I especially recommend for beginners), the article, "Evaluating Suppliers," on GlobalSources.com shares what to look for when auditing factories. It provides specific criteria to help assess supplier performance, focusing on the evaluation of important benchmarks such as quality of service and goods. Here is some information from that article:

1. Is the company in compliance with local labor laws? Does the factory comply with ISO 9001 and SA 8000 standards?
    a. Facilities: Areas for manufacturing, testing, packing, and loading
    b. Processes: Lead-time estimates, control of records and procurement system
    c. Management: Credentials and workflow systems
    d. Social compliance: Child labor, working hours, and wages
2. Does the company have all the documentation that your lawyers are requesting or that you require?
    a. Export license
    b. Testing certificates
    c. Industry standards
    d. MNC certification (if applicable)
3. Visit the factory yourself.
    a. Spend more time on the production floor than anywhere else.
    b. Bring your own interpreter, and visit as many sites as possible.
    c. What is its current condition with regard to capacity, finances, and staff?
    d. Find out:
        When the factory is most busy and whether this is in conflict with your schedule
        How much of the production is subcontracted
        How the factory controls IP and nonconforming products

4. Inspect workflow systems for efficiency, and check whether they are actually practiced.

5. Test your supplier's understanding of your product's requirements. Request that samples are sent to you to your exact specifications (pay if necessary).

6. Evaluate the factory's quality system.

a. Does the factory have a clear list of all desired characteristics of a product before production starts?

b. Is it clearly specified how each characteristic should be measured?

c. Are approved samples available to workers in production and quality control (QC) areas?

d. How does the factory evaluate and select material suppliers?

e. Does it communicate the requirements accurately to material suppliers?

f. Does it check whether a purchased product is up to specifications? How?

g. Does it send samples for laboratory tests? How often and for what tests?

h. Are materials stored properly?

i. Does the factory give clear procedures to each worker and for each job (including the QC staff)?

j. How does it validate that each production process achieves the desired results?

k. Does it carry out in-process QC? On what proportion of products? What does it do with the data collected this way (corrective/preventive actions)? What happens to pieces found to be defective?

l. How does it ensure that measuring instruments are available and used correctly?

m. Do the operators control their own work? Do they receive regular training?

n. Are materials delivered directly to subcontractors? How are they checked?

o. How does the factory control the work of subcontractor(s)?

BETTER SUPPLY-CHAIN MANAGEMENT

p. What does it check about the subcontractors' operations?

q. What proportion of products is checked? How are they checked? Does the check include packing?

r. Is there one last inspection based on the acceptance quality limit (AQL) statistics? Based on what level of AQL?

s. What happens when nonconformities are detected?

Not everyone has to look at his or her supplier benchmark evaluation in exactly this way, but it's a helpful place to start. Think about which criterion is most useful for your business's products.

Mark Taylor, consultant for growing businesses and third-sector organizations, explains how he evaluates suppliers and product lines:

Set up a product/vendor rating system. The idea here is to set criteria that are important to you (e.g., quality, price, ethical sourcing, etc.) and have a scoring system—spreadsheets are quite helpful here. Evaluate each of your major suppliers/product lines against these criteria, and select those that score best. This seems to work well but does not necessarily give you "tablets of stone"— if something doesn't sit right, revisit your criteria and scores. If that fails, just go with your instinct—I think the heart should always overrule the head!

Mark's method is helpful, especially when choosing suppliers in the beginning. However, it can be adapted to an evaluation system further along as well. To maintain a quality relationship with suppliers, perform yearly evaluations to ensure that you're getting the best service from them.

Suppliers' Credit Reports, Credit Scores, Certifications, and Insurance
Some other ways to evaluate suppliers are through their Dun & Bradstreet numbers, as well as their Experian and Equifax credit reports. Verify the supplier's website domain registration and phone number. The supplier should be willing to provide this information. It's also helpful to find out what other types of certificates the supplier has and whether its merchandise has been tested. Some common certifications

for overseas suppliers include Société Générale de Surveillance (SGS) reports and reports from www.consumerreports.org. These are two big boards that govern product safety and are trusted sources.

You also always should ask whether suppliers have insurance on their products. It will protect you when selling them. If a customer gets hurt due to a manufacturing flaw, you need to have protection to make sure that you aren't the one being sued. You will want to go back to your supplier and confirm that it is liable and responsible for these types of issues. The supplier should have the proper manufacturing certifications and insurance on its merchandise that covers these types of mishaps. However, if you are manufacturing your own products, this does not replace the importance of carrying your own product-liability coverage. Most of the larger buyers at big-box retail chains will require you to have coverage if you want to work with them.

Cindy Teasdale McGowan, owner of Makaboo Personalized Gifts, explains why it's important to work with suppliers that have manufacturing certifications and are informed about the safety of their products:

A customer of mine had signed up for federally regulated alerts for children's product recalls. He saw a supplier that I had been working with and forwarded me the alert. In the e-mail I saw a recall for a holiday set of boy's pajamas from this company. I immediately contacted the supplier, telling them about the e-mail, and they were very wishy-washy about what we had to do and how to move forward. We had to pull items from our stock and take down all the lifestyle photography that featured the item from my website. This rendered a ton of photos unusable, even though they featured other products that were selling great. And on top of that, we had to pay the cost of shipping the items back to the manufacturer. They wouldn't give us a refund. Now that I have more experience, I know that a more professional supplier would have been proactive about alerting me of these issues and would have made changes to the product before getting in trouble with the government. It wasn't as bad as it could have been because it was a voluntary recall and no child got hurt, but it wasn't a pleasant experience.

Cindy's situation shows that working with the right supplier is important not only for avoiding hassles and protecting your finances but also for your reputation with customers. To avoid these types of issues, ask suppliers about their merchandising and support policies. Before you do business with a supplier, evaluate its ability to perform customer service. Ask your supplier the following questions:

- What is your returns policy?
- Do you give discounts on damaged goods?
- What is your dispute-resolution policy?

The answers to these questions help you to review your suppliers and choose trustworthy partners with whom you can have a strong relationship. You also will be able to avoid experiences such as Cindy's.

Pros and Cons of Evaluating Your Suppliers
Having formal evaluations and checking for credibility of suppliers can be time-consuming and costly for small businesses or entrepreneurs (especially for those of you who have never done this before). However, I hope that you see why it's well worth the effort and understand that you will learn a lot from the process. When you take the time to do this type of due diligence, it teaches you important information about your partner's business (and your own business). You will save yourself from many potential hazards and will know how to make instantaneous business decisions related to the suppliers and vendors with whom you're working. It provides you with hard data that help you to make important business decisions related to your supply chain.

. . .

Everyone has different evaluation standards, and each business has to invent its own way of managing its relationships with suppliers. Every business's needs are different, and each supplier is unique. It takes time to develop your business instinct, but it's important that you take the time to do it through these types of practices.

Formal evaluation time also can be used to help you build and strengthen relationships with suppliers. Twistlets cofounder Dominique Castro shared with me the more fun side of auditing factories:

> Something that brought me close to my supplier from the beginning was their love for Americans and American culture. When I visited my factory during the auditing process, it was not easy to communicate with them because they were shy when speaking English. However, this all changed when the Black Eyed Peas song, "Boom Boom Pow," came on in the factory. We all started singing! It went from no communication to letting our inhibitions go and having a great time together. They became more relaxed, and we even had a full-on conversation about Lady Gaga. I realized that there are certain things that bring us together—music being one of them. If you connect with your factory personnel on a personal level, you'll find that people start to work for you with joy and are more supportive throughout the process. After that experience, I even started receiving responses to e-mails during the day (which is the middle of the night in China). When you become important to them, they will go the extra mile for you.

TIP

If you're still in the beginning phases of choosing a partner and formal evaluations are too time-consuming or expensive right now, at least take the time to get trade references from potential suppliers. Have suppliers give you references from some companies they're doing business with. In this way, you can cross-reference and verify that they have some good long-standing accounts. Make sure that their business has been functioning for a long time and that it's doing well.

Relationship-Management Guidelines: How to Raise Issues, Know When to Drop Suppliers, and Protect Yourself

Working with suppliers is just like working with an employee or a partner. You don't want to yell at them or waste energy being mad when you have a problem. Usually, there's just a simple misunderstanding, miscommunication, or a discussion needs to take place. In business, most people do not have bad intentions. If you start assuming that they do, the paranoia can bring on its own problems.

When there's a big issue such as late shipping, poor product quality, slow e-mail responses, or packaging problems and you decide to make a complaint about it, the last thing you want to do is to take things out of perspective and allow issues to become bigger than they really are. When problems arise, it's best to keep a journal and/or document with concerns in a spreadsheet. In this way, you can pick a good time to go over each item and have a review.

I suggest having a monthly review with your suppliers. You should start the review by focusing on what is going well in the relationship and then state your issues one by one in a listed order. Here's an example of the vernacular to use when addressing problems: "Hey Charlie, you know, I really think that we are making some progress. The last couple of shipments and orders have been going great. However, there are a couple of areas that I would like to address, and here are all my points. . . . " By approaching the issues in this manner, you won't bombard your partner with negativity and cause a difficult working relationship. You'll also have a better chance of refraining from getting overly upset with him or her. If you complain about issues in the moment, there is a higher likelihood that you will stay something in a way that you don't mean or blow a situation out of proportion. This only creates a tense, uncomfortable working relationship with your vendors, and you don't want that type of relationship; these partners are important for your success.

Instead of getting upset, stay in control and use warnings. There are ways to overcome challenges. You can turn your disappointment into opportunity by addressing issues one by one and explaining that if they continue, you will have to find another supplier. Suppliers want your business and want to please you, but they are people and can make mistakes. If they are a good supplier, they will do what they can to rectify the issue quickly once they understand your concerns.

Bruce Rubin, principal at BHR Global, explains the importance of addressing issues:

> Don't let issues fester—it will kill the relationship. Take into consideration cultural differences, but remember that a relationship is a relationship, and people are people (regardless of where they are located). Treat your suppliers like people, and you may find that they may just need to make some changes to their methodology to solve seemingly difficult problems.

However, if suppliers don't make changes and you have addressed the issues in a calm and controlled way, then you need to rid yourself of these bad suppliers fast. If an issue is repetitive and your partner does not make the effort to fix it, don't waste your time in a situation that doesn't work. Don't convince yourself that it's not a big deal because you are losing customers, and your product or service becomes low quality. Don't put up with problems that persist even once you have addressed them several times. There are many suppliers out there. Just go on TopTen Wholesale.com or Manufacturer.com, and you'll see that they are replaceable.

• • •

At TopTenWholesale.com and Manufacturer.com we have a saying, "Hire slow and fire fast." When you make a sourcing decision, you're making a decision that will have a major impact on your business. It's something that you want to view as a long-term investment. It's a relationship that you need to foster with a lot of time and energy. If you realize that your partner is no longer worthy of your business, don't waste your energy trying to make it better. You should eliminate that supplier quickly because staying in a negative work-related situation usually only gets worse and can cause some negative repercussions. Albert Einstein made this very clear when he said, "Insanity is doing the same thing, over and over again, but expecting different results."

Shreyans Parekh, cofounder of Koyal Wholesale, adds that you need to operate with high-standard companies whether locally or abroad: "If you're not satisfied with the product quality or service that you're receiving, then you need to drop the manufacturer. Be aware of what is going on and constantly reevaluate them."

TIP

One easy way to monitor suppliers is by using Google Alerts (which you may remember from Chapter 2). Google Alerts allow you to discover more about your suppliers' companies. When you decide to work with a supplier, make sure that you create a Google account and set up Google Alerts following your supplier's website address, company name, and names of the executives of the business. These are very easy to create. All you need is a Google account that you can find at https://accounts.google.com/NewAccount.

By monitoring suppliers, you will know more about how they work. By having Google Alerts, you can see whether people launch complaints against them on message boards. The supplier could have a complaint filed against it on RipOffReport.com or on a forum. Some other sites that I recommend scouring are RipOffReport.com and Yelp.com. You can't believe everything you read on them, but they can be helpful. Also, for finding information about international suppliers, I recommend that you try TopTenWholesale Answers or the Alibaba forums. And don't forget to check to see whether the supplier has a business page on Facebook, or is active on Twitter. There's a lot of market research that you can do to know more about suppliers and their daily practices.

The Importance of Written Agreements

It's important to have written agreements. Nondisclosure agreements (NDAs), purchase orders, brokering merchandise from a supplier, and pricing for the new quarter all need to be put down on paper. In the retail and wholesale business (especially when sourcing from overseas), you need to protect yourself from misunderstandings. There's nothing more dangerous than simply shaking hands, making oral agreements with suppliers, and assuming that you are covered if anything goes wrong. You need contracts.

TIP

I highly recommend nondisclosure agreements (NDAs) to protect innovative ideas. You never want to do business with anyone who won't sign an NDA when developing a new, innovative product.

Michael Zakkour, principal at Technomic Asia (a wholly owned subsidiary of Tompkins International), also confirms that contracts are very important:

Relationships with suppliers should be based on contracts. Don't listen to people (whether they are based overseas or in the United States) who say that contracts in China don't matter due to the fact that it's a relationship-based society. Yes, it is a relationship-based society and you get ahead through relationships, but you don't do transactional deals on a relationship basis. You do them through contracts. Contracts define the relationship between you and the manufacturer and are how problems need to be resolved. Also, keep in mind that your purchase order (PO) is not a contract! You would be surprised at how many small, medium, and large companies operate on the assumption that it is. If something goes wrong, your PO will not give you recourse resolution. Technically, it's not a legal document and will not withstand in courts.

Michael's advice may pertain to China, but having contracts, NDAs, and written documents is important no matter where you're doing business.

Top 10 Recap: Ways to Cultivate Relationships and Get Past Cultural/Language Barriers

In many places throughout this book I have discussed the importance of cultivating relationships with suppliers. Whether they're located domestically or internationally, I hope that you understand that it's important to get to know them and make them feel like your partners. They are vital to the success of your business. Also, if they are located abroad, you have to remember that getting past cultural and language barriers is not easy. However, with some effort, it can be done and is an important part of working with global suppliers.

• • •

Let's quickly review some of the top 10 most important—yet simple to apply—tips that can help you to maintain a strong working relationship with domestic and international suppliers:

1. *Create face-to-face networking opportunities.* Find out what trade shows your partners go to, and see whether you can meet them there or for dinner afterward. If possible, I highly recommend going (or sending someone to go) to the factory that will be producing your products. Nothing can replace a face-to-face onsite meeting.

2. *Communicate often, frequently, and clearly.* Be wary of using difficult language when writing to nonnative speakers. Alain Stambouli, owner of Via Trading, recommends "keeping com-

munication simple and straightforward. Avoid using colloquial terms or slang in correspondence. Take the time to properly check understanding if you are in doubt."

3. *Participate with suppliers in social media.* Make sure that when you are searching for them on the Internet you find their business's page on Facebook. See if they are on Twitter or LinkedIn, and connect with them.

4. *Know your partners' schedules.* Be polite and respectful of the holidays and working hours of the country where the person you are working with lives. You don't want to contact someone at 3:00 a.m. their time (unless it's by e-mail) or when they're on vacation. Dominique Castro, cofounder of Twistlets, recommends this handy website that can help you find out various countries' holiday schedules: www.sourcingjournalonline.com/international-holidays.

5. *Be patient and understanding.* We are all human beings doing our best, but sometimes we make mistakes. Being patient and expecting that your partners want a healthy working relationship with you helps.

6. *Use contracts and written agreements.* Get responsibilities written down in black and white so that there is no confusion about who will be doing what throughout the process.

7. *Have a product/vendor rating system.* This will help you to choose which partners to work with and/or stay on top of the relationship. You will learn a lot about yourself and your partners. This will help you to make business decisions more quickly and clearly.

8. *Be honest and respectful.* What we learned in kindergarten can go a long way (even as we become big-shot, successful entrepreneurs). Nothing makes people more willing to do their best than a little kindness and integrity. Be HIP!

9. *Understand the culture you want to work with.* Bruce Rubin, principal at BHR Global, agrees:

Try and understand the culture of the supplier you want to work with. Do homework on the culture. Talk to people who have gone to the country so that you don't embarrass yourself, and don't ask the wrong questions. Understand that what works in your country doesn't necessarily work overseas.

10. *Go with your gut.* Relationships are relationships, and people are people. Listen to your inner voice. Whether your intuition is telling you to back away from the partnership or stay, follow its lead.

Conclusion

Throughout this chapter, you have learned how building and nurturing strong relationships are about more than just choosing partners you get along with. You understand that they deal with making good business decisions that will help you to run your supply chain more successfully. You're aware of the criteria that help you to evaluate whether or not suppliers are right for you, and that also helps you to manage relationships. You have learned how to communicate issues to suppliers and how to decide whether it's time to move on and find a new partner. Whether you choose a local or overseas supplier, you now understand how to build and maintain a successful working relationship with them. This will keep your supply chain healthy and drive the success of your company forward.

Some Parting Words While Looking Ahead

You have now successfully completed a giant leap toward becoming an entrepreneur or have found new and innovative ways to approach challenging issues in your already established business. Whether you're sourcing products for a retail or wholesale business or launching your own product line, you are now aware of the tools and the people that can make it happen. I've met many experts along the way, and you have learned heaps of insider secrets and strategies. I want to congratulate you on taking the time to access this knowledge. It will help lead to your success. You now know how to use the most important resources for global trade and how to find the best suppliers to source from. Remember, money is made when sourcing products, not when selling them. This is why building strong relationships with your trading partners is paramount for your success.

But your journey doesn't stop here. This is just the beginning! I encourage you to put this information into practice. Network with industry peers, go to trade shows, join the community on TopTenWholesale.com, and speak to manufacturers' reps. You have all the knowledge that you need to make your dreams become a reality. You just need to go out and make it happen! It's okay to move forward in baby steps, and you always have this book as a guide to help if you get stuck. But I can't jump out of the pages and do it for you. You need to make this happen yourself. I wish nothing more than for your ability to use this information and thrive in the wholesale/retail industry. Good luck to you and your business, and may you find the sourcing partners that lead to your success.

Appendix A
Resources for Global Trade

WITH THE help of Roni Miller Start, department chair of apparel industry management at the Fashion Institute of Design and Merchandising (FIDM), I have created a list of the best resources for entrepreneurs and global trade. These websites cover a variety of topics from news about small-business loans to information about Asia-Pacific trade agreements.

Information for Entrepreneurs and Startups

Association of Small Business Development Centers: www.asbdc-us.org. Provides small businesses and entrepreneurs in the United States and its territories with assistance, education, and consulting.

Bureau of Labor Statistics: http://stats.bls.gov/audience/business.htm. Provides statistics that help you to find new markets for your products, negotiate contracts, compare your business with others in the industry, and assess employment costs.

BussinessUSA: http://business.usa.gov/. A one-stop shop for everything related to business in the United States.

California Fashion Association (CFA): www.calfashion.org/index.
php?option=com_content&task=view&id=30&Itemid. Founded in
1995, CFA is a nonprofit public-benefit corporation that deals with
issues affecting the apparel and textile community of California.

City of Los Angeles, Office of the Mayor Business Resources: http://mayor
.lacity.org/Services/BusinessResources/index.htm. Provides
information about LA city jobs, business taxes, development,
permits, and more.

Export-Import Bank of the United States: www.exim.gov/smallbusiness/.
Provides small businesses with global access through increased
financing for exports and the creation of jobs in the United States.

The Fashion Center: www.fashioncenter.com/business/entrepreneurs,
http://www.ftasc.org/. Provides resources for fashion businesses (from
designers to store owners) in midtown Manhattan's fashion district.

Federal Trade Commission: www.ftc.gov/oia/about.shtm. Develops
policies that protect consumers in the international marketplace.
It focuses on emerging technologies and e-commerce and works
with international organizations such as the Working Party on
Information Security and Privacy of the OECD, Committee on
Consumer Policy of the OECD, the APEC Telecommunication
and Information Working Group, and the APEC Electronic
Commerce Steering Group and its Data Privacy Subgroup.

Internal Revenue Service (IRS): www.irs.gov/businesses. Hosts small-
business tax workshops and webinars and provides tax-related
information for starting, operating, or closing a business.

International Factoring Association: www.factoring.org/. Provides
training, information, and acts as a resource for the factoring
community.

Los Angeles Business Assistance Virtual Network: www.labavn.org/. The
Business Assistance Virtual Network (BAVN) is a free service
from the City of Los Angeles Office of Small Business Services and
Minority Business Opportunity Committee. It provides information
about all bid opportunities offered by the City of Los Angeles and
certified subcontractors to complement project bids.

Los Angeles Works: www.losangelesworks.org/whyLaWorks/the-la-economy.cfm. A resource for existing businesses, as well as for people who want to start businesses in Los Angeles.

Minority Business Development Agency (MBDA): www.mbda.gov/main/offices. Funds a network of minority business centers located throughout the nation that provide minority entrepreneurs with one-on-one assistance in marketing, writing business plans, management, technical assistance, and financial planning.

National Association of Manufacturers: www.Nam.org. A newsroom hosted by the U.S. National Association of Manufacturers, which shares manufacturing industry–related news.

Overseas Private Investment Corporation (OPIC): www.opic.gov/doing-business-us/small-business-center/small-business-guide. Helps businesses apply for loans and find financing options through its "Small and Medium Enterprises (SMEs) Business Guide." The guide acts as a navigation tool and provides other helpful online resources.

STOPfakes: www.stopfakes.gov. STOPfakes is a one-stop shop for U.S. government resources and tools on intellectual property rights (IPRs). It assists and educates small and medium-sized enterprises (SMEs), consumers, government officials, and the general public about IRPs.

Trade Show Exhibitors Association: www.tsea.org/. Provides knowledge to management and marketing professionals who promote and sell products through face-to-face marketing. This is also a great resource for finding trade shows.

U.S. Patent and Trademark Office: www.uspto.gov. Registers trademarks and protects intellectual property (IP) for U.S. entrepreneurs and innovators worldwide.

U.S. Small Business Administration: www.sba.gov/. The SBA has resources and information for starting and managing businesses, getting loans and grants, registering for government contracting, and receiving business counseling and training.

Global Trade Resources

American Apparel & Footwear Association: www.wewear.org. A national trade association that represents apparel, footwear, and other sewn-products companies and suppliers that compete in the global marketplace.

Asia-Pacific Research and Training Network on Trade: www.unescap .org/tid/artnet/about.asp. Aims to increase the amount of relevant trade research in the Asia-Pacific Region through enhanced research mechanisms, increased interactions between researchers and policy makers, and specific activities catering to research institutions from the least developed countries in this region.

CBP.gov: www.cbp.gov/xp/cgov/about/. Helps to facilitate lawful international travel and trade.

Cybex's International Trade Resources: www.cybex.in/International-Trade-Resources/Default.aspx. Provides Indian trade data as well as country codes, exchange rates, Incoterms, Indian embassy information, export promotion councils, and more.

International Chamber of Commerce: http://iccwbo.org/about-icc/. Helps businesses understand the world economy and facilitates international trade and investment. It's also famous for creating the Incoterms, which are common terms used in contracts when selling international goods.

International Trade Administration: http://www.Trade.gov. Ensures fair trade through trade laws and agreements, promotes trade and investment, and strengthens U.S. businesses' competition in the global business environment.

Los Angeles Customs Brokers and Freight Forwarders Association: www.lacbffa.org/. As the premier organization in southern California for international trade, this association represents common business interests of customs brokers and freight forwarders in dealing with carriers, government, industry, and one another.

Manufacturer.com: www.manufacturer.com/. The premier global online business-to-business marketplace where buyers and suppliers connect and profit. Billions of dollars of general merchandise, apparel, and fashion accessories are sourced through Manufacturer. com as millions of buyers throughout the world connect directly to suppliers in China, India, the United States, and dozens of other countries.

Manufacturing.net: www.Manufacturing.net. Shares manufacturing industry–related news, opinions, and trends related to the global manufacturing community.

Office of the U.S. Trade Representative: www.ustr.gov/about-us/mission. Develops and coordinates U.S. international trade, investment policy, and oversees negotiations with other countries.

Port of Los Angeles: www.portoflosangeles.org/business/trade.asp. Hosts a workshop called Trade Connect that covers the basics of exporting (i.e., costs, risks, and steps), the basics of the commercial transaction, and logistics, finding overseas markets, trade financing, and documentation.

Sourcing Online Journal: www.SourcingJournalOnline.com. A global news resource with information for business executives who want to know about supply-chain-related topics within the soft-goods and textile industry.

TopTenWholesale.com: www.toptenwholesale.com/. A vertical search engine that connects buyers of general-merchandise wholesale products to manufacturers, importers, distributors, auctioneers, independent retailers, flea marketers, drop shippers, and any reseller of new and closeouts merchandise.

Tradeology: http://Blog.trade.gov. The official blog of the International Trade Administration, which discusses international trade laws and agreements.

U.S. Census Bureau Foreign Trade: www.census.gov/foreign-trade/. Provides official U.S. export and import statistics, export-regulation information, commodity classifications, and other data related to trade.

U.S. Department of Commerce: www.commerce.gov/. Helps to drive competitiveness in the global marketplace by promoting economic growth, job creation, and sustainable development. The site is also linked to other helpful resources related to global trade.

U.S. Department of Labor Bureau of International Labor Laws: www .dol.gov/ILAB/programs/otla/. Ensures that workers are treated fairly all over the world. It improves working conditions, raises living standards, protects workers' rights, and addresses the exploitation of children and other vulnerable populations in the workplace.

U.S. International Trade Commission: www.usitc.gov/. Contributes to the development of sound and informed U.S. trade policy and implements U.S. trade laws. This resource also provides helpful information such as the Official Harmonized Tariff Schedule, which is the primary resource for determining tariff classifications for goods imported into the United States.

U.S. Commercial Service: www.BuyUsa.gov. Helps companies from the United States find international business partners in markets worldwide.

U.S. Trade and Development Agency: www.ustda.gov/businessopps/ smbusinesses.asp. Provides companies with opportunities to export their goods and services for development projects in emerging economies.

USAID: www.usaid.gov/what-we-do/economic-growth-and-trade. Develops partnerships with countries that are committed to enabling private-sector investment. It promotes sustained economic growth by opening new markets for American goods, promoting trade overseas, and creating jobs in the United States.

WorldCity: www.worldcityweb.com/customs-districts/los-angeles. A media company that focuses on the impact of the global economy on local businesses, local communities, and globally focused executives. Its two primary areas of focus are import-export trade data and the multinationals in the Greater Miami Area. It also provides current trade data.

World Customs Organization (WCO): www.wcoomd.org/home_about _us.htm. Works on the development of global standards, trade supply-chain security, simplification of customs procedures, enhancement of customs enforcement, facilitation of international trade, anticounterfeiting and piracy initiatives, public-private partnerships, integrity promotion, and sustainable global customs capacity-building programs. Also administers technical aspects of the WTO Agreements on Rules of Origin and Customs Valuation.

World Integrated Trade Solution (WITS): http://wits.worldbank.org/wits/. Software developed by the World Bank that gives you access to major international trade, tariffs, and nontariff data compilations such as imports and exports by detailed commodity and partner country.

XE: www.xe.com/ucc/. A free and live currency-converter widget.

Appendix B

The Jargon behind International Trade

THE FOLLOWING definitions can serve as your own personal translator whenever you encounter jargon that you aren't familiar with while sourcing products. This resource covers terms for sourcing, international trade, the wholesale industry, packing, and shipping.

Sourcing Terms

B2B trade platforms   Business-to-business vertical search engines that connect buyers and sellers in global and domestic trade. These online marketplaces provide tools that are necessary to facilitate communication between retailers/resellers and wholesalers/manufacturers.

MOQ   The smallest quantity of a product that a supplier requires you to buy in a single purchase.

Product sourcing   The act of finding products from wholesalers or manufacturers to resell through a business.

RFQ   Request for quotation, a business process that invites suppliers to bid on specific products or services. It allows suppliers to provide quotations for their goods and services.

International Trade Terms

I have hand selected the most relevant international trade terms for your sourcing purposes from the Export Bureau's *A–Z Dictionary of Export, Trade and Shipping Terms*. To find any additional definitions that I haven't included here, I encourage you to visit the Export Bureau's website at www.exportbureau.com/dictionary.html.

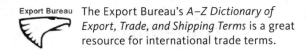 **Export Bureau**   The Export Bureau's *A–Z Dictionary of Export, Trade, and Shipping Terms* is a great resource for international trade terms.

Acceptance   The act of a drawee acknowledging in writing on the face of a draft, payable at a fixed or determinable future date, that he or she will pay the draft at maturity.

Acceptance draft   A sight draft, documents against acceptance. See *Sight draft, Documents against acceptance.*

Airway bill   The carrying agreement between shipper and air carrier that is obtained from the airline used to ship the goods.

All-risks clause   An insurance provision that provides additional coverage to an open cargo policy, usually for an additional premium. Contrary to its name, the clause does not protect against all risks. The more common perils it does cover are theft, pilferage, nondelivery, freshwater damage, contact with other cargo, breakage, and leakage. Inherent vice, loss of market, and losses caused by delay are not covered.

ATA carnet   Customs document that enables one to carry or send goods temporarily into certain foreign countries without paying duties or posting bonds.

Authority to pay   A document comparable with a revocable letter of credit but under whose terms the authority to pay the seller stems from the buyer rather than from a bank.

Balance of trade   The balance between a country's exports and imports.

Beneficiary   The person in whose favor a letter of credit is issued or a draft is drawn.

Bill of exchange   See *Draft.*

Bill of lading   A document that provides the terms of the contract between the shipper and the transportation company to move freight between stated points at a specified charge.

Bonded warehouse   A building authorized by customs authorities for the storage of goods without payment of duties until removal.

Brussels Tariff Nomenclature   See *Nomenclature of the Customs Cooperation Council.*

Buying agent   An agent who buys in this country for foreign importers, especially for such large foreign users as mines, railroads, governments, and public utilities. Synonymous with *purchasing agent.*

C. & F. (cost and freight)   Same as C.I.F., except that insurance is covered by the buyer.

Carrier   A transportation line that hauls cargo.

Certificate of free sale   A certificate, required by some foreign governments, stating that the goods for export (if products are under the jurisdiction of the U.S. Federal Food and Drug Administration) are acceptable for sale in the United States, that is, that the products are sold freely, without restriction. The FDA will issue shippers a *letter of comment* to satisfy foreign requests or regulations.

Certificate of inspection   A document in which certification is made as to the good condition of the merchandise immediately prior to shipment. The buyer usually designates the inspecting organization, which is typically an independent inspection firm or government body.

Certificate of manufacture   A statement by a producer, sometimes notarized, that certifies that manufacturing has been completed and that the goods are at the disposal of the buyer.

Certificate of origin   A document in which certification is made as to the country of origin of the merchandise.

C.F.R. (cost and freight) and C.I.F. (cost, insurance, and freight)   Indicates that the seller will deliver the goods onto a vessel and pay all the normal charges to get the cargo to the named seaport. The buyer assumes all risks from the time the cargo is placed onto the vessel at the seaport of loading. C.I.F. also indicates that the seller arranges for insurance as an automatic condition of the contract.

Chamber of Commerce   An association of businesspeople whose purpose is to promote commercial and industrial interests in the community.

C.I.F. (cost, insurance, and freight)   A pricing term under which the seller pays all expenses involved in the placing of merchandise on board a carrier and in addition prepays the freight and insures the goods to an agreed destination.

Clean bill of lading   A bill of lading signed by the transportation company indicating that the shipment has been received in good condition with no irregularities in the packing or general condition of all or any part of the shipment. See *Foul bill of lading*.

Collection   The procedure involved in a bank's collecting money for a seller against a draft drawn on a buyer abroad, usually through a correspondent bank.

Collection papers   The documents submitted, usually with a draft or against a letter of credit, for payment of an export shipment.

Commercial attaché   The commercial expert on the diplomatic staff of his or her country's embassy or large consulate in a foreign country.

Commercial invoice   A trade invoice.

Commission agent   See *Foreign sales representative*.

Commission representative   See *Foreign sales representative*.

Conference line A member of a steamship conference. See *Steamship conference*.

Confirmed letter of credit Issued by a bank abroad whose validity and terms are confirmed to the beneficiary in the United States by a U.S. bank.

Consignee The person, firm, or representative to whom a seller or shipper sends merchandise and who, on presentation of the necessary documents, is recognized as the owner of the merchandise for the purpose of the payment of customs duties. This term is also used as applying to one to whom goods are shipped, usually at the shipper's risk, when an outright sale has not been made. See *Consignment*.

Consignment A term pertaining to merchandise shipped to a consignee abroad when an actual purchase has not been made, under an agreement by which the consignee is obligated to sell the goods for the account of the consignor and to remit proceeds as goods are sold.

Consul A government official residing in a foreign country who is charged with the representation of the interests of his or her country and its nationals.

Consular invoice A detailed statement regarding the character of goods shipped, duly certified by the consul of the importing country at the port of shipment.

Contingency insurance Insurance taken out by a shipper (supplementary to insurance taken out by the consignee abroad), especially to cover shipments made on a C. & F. basis.

Correspondent bank A bank that is a depository for another bank, accepting deposits and collecting items for its bank depositor.

Country of origin The country in which a product or commodity is manufactured or produced.

Credit-risk insurance A form of insurance that protects the seller against loss due to default on the part of the buyer. See *FCIA*.

Customs   The agency or procedure for collecting duties imposed by a country on imports or exports.

D/A   See *Documents against acceptance*.

D/P   See *Documents against payment*.

Delivered at frontier   The seller's obligations are not fulfilled when the goods have arrived at the frontier but before the "customs border" of the country named in the sales contract.

Delivered duty paid   While the term *ex works* signifies the seller's minimum obligation, the term *delivered duty paid*, when followed by words naming the buyer's premises, denotes the other extreme—the seller's maximum obligation—and may be used irrespective of the mode of transport.

Delivered duty unpaid   The seller must deliver the goods to the named destination and is responsible for all costs involved in transportation, including exportation. The buyer handles the import formalities.

D.E.Q. (delivered ex quay)   Indicates that the seller must deliver the goods onto the quay (dock or wharf), having cleared the goods for import and paid all taxes, duties, etc. applicable to that clearance.

Delivery point   See *Specific delivery point*.

Demurrage   Excess time taken for loading or unloading a vessel as a result of acts of a shipper. The shipping company assesses the charges.

DISC   See *Domestic international sales corporation*.

Discount (financial)   A deduction from the face value of commercial paper such as bills of exchange in consideration of receipt of cash by the seller before maturity date.

Discrepancy—letter of credit   When documents presented do not conform to the terms of the letter of credit, it is referred to as a *discrepancy*.

Distributor   A firm that sells directly for a manufacturer, usually on an exclusive basis for a specified territory, and that maintains an inventory on hand.

Dock receipt   A receipt issued by an ocean carrier or its agent acknowledging that a shipment has been delivered and received at the dock or warehouse of the carrier.

Documentary credit   See *Letter of credit (commercial)*.

Documentary draft   A draft to which documents are attached.

Documentation/documents   See *Shipping documents*.

Documents against acceptance (D/A)   A type of payment for goods in which the documents transferring title to the goods are not given to the buyer until he or she has accepted the draft issued against him or her.

Documents against payment (D/P)   A type of payment for goods in which the documents transferring title to the goods are not given to the buyer until he or she has paid the value of a draft issued against him or her.

Domestic international sales corporation (DISC)   An export sales corporation set up by a U.S. company under U.S. government authorization to promote exports from the United States by giving the exporter economic advantages not available outside such authorization.

Draft   The same as a *bill of exchange*. A written order for a certain sum of money to be transferred on a certain date from the person who owes the money or agrees to make the payment (the drawee) to the creditor to whom the money is owed (the drawer of the draft). See *Date draft*, *Documentary draft*, *Sight draft*, and *Time draft*.

Drawback (import)   The repayment (up to 99 percent) of customs duties paid on merchandise that later is exported as part of a finished product. It refers also to a refund of a domestic tax that has been paid on exportation of imported merchandise.

Drawee   One on whom a draft is drawn and who owes the stated amount. See *Draft*.

Drawer   One who draws a draft and receives payment. See *Draft*.

Duty   The tax imposed by a government on merchandise imported from another country.

EMC   Export management company.

ETC   Export trading company.

Ex (point of origin)   A pricing term under which the seller's only responsibility is to clear the goods for export and make them available to the buyer at an agreed on location (e.g., factory, warehouse, ship, etc.). The buyer then bears the full cost and risk involved in transporting the goods to his or her desired location. Other terms used are *ex works*, *ex ship*, and *ex quay*.

Exchange permit   A government permit sometimes required of an importer to enable him or her to convert his or her own country's currency into a foreign currency with which to pay a seller in another country.

Exchange regulations/restrictions   Restrictions imposed by an importing country to protect its foreign-exchange reserves. See *Exchange permit*.

Eximbank   The Export-Import Bank of the United States in Washington. See *Guide to Export Assistance*.

Excise tax   A domestic tax assessed on the manufacture, sale, or use of a commodity within a country. Usually refundable if the product is exported.

Expiration date   The final date on which the presentation of documents and drawing of drafts under a letter of credit may be made.

Export   To send goods to a foreign country or overseas territory.

Export broker   One who brings together the exporter and importer for a fee and then withdraws from the transaction.

Export declaration   See *Shipper's export declaration*.

Export license   A government permit required to export certain products to certain destinations.

Export management company (EMC)   A firm that acts as a local export sales agent for several noncompeting manufacturers. (Term synonymous with *manufacturer's export agent*.)

Export merchant   A producer or merchant who sells directly to a foreign purchaser without going through an intermediate such as an export broker.

E.X.W. (ex works)   Indicates that the buyer is responsible for cargo when it's available at the seller's factory.

F.A.S. (free alongside), as in "F.A.S. (vessel)"   A pricing term under which the seller must deliver the goods to a pier and place them within reach of the ship's loading equipment.

F.C.A. (free carrier at)   Indicates that the seller delivers the goods to the named place free of any transportation cost, having cleared the cargo for export. The seller accepts transportation costs, risks, and responsibilities until the cargo is handed over at the named place.

FCIA   Foreign Credit Insurance Association.

Floating policy   See *Open policy*.

F.O.B. (free on board), as in "F.O.B. (vessel)"   A pricing term under which the seller must deliver the goods on board the ship at the point named at his or her own expense. Similar terms are *F.O.B. (destination)* and *F.O.B. (named point of exportation)*.

FOR (free on rail) and FOT (free on truck)   These terms are synonymous because the word *truck* relates to the railway wagons. They should only be used when the goods are to be carried by rail.

Foreign sales representative   A representative or agent residing in a foreign country who acts as a salesperson for a U.S. manufacturer, usually for a commission. Sometimes referred to as a *sales agent* or *commission agent*. See *Representative*.

Foreign trade zone An area where goods of foreign origin may be brought in for re-export or transshipment without the payment of customs duty.

Foul bill of lading A receipt for goods issued by a carrier bearing a notation that the outward containers or goods have been damaged. See *Clean bill of lading*.

Free carrier (named place) The seller must clear the goods for export and deliver them to a carrier at a specific point determined by the buyer. The buyer then bears all costs and risks of transporting the goods to the desired destination. Also see *Named point* and *Specific delivery point*.

Free port An area generally encompassing a port and its surrounding locality into which goods may enter duty-free or subject only to minimal revenue tariffs.

Free sale See *Certificate of free sale*.

Freight carriage (paid to) Like C. & F., this means that the seller pays the freight for the carriage of the goods to the named destination. However, the risk of loss of or damage to the goods, as well as the risk of any cost increases, is transferred from the seller to the buyer when the goods have been delivered into the custody of the first carrier and not at the ship's rail.

Freight carriage (and insurance paid to) Like freight or carriage paid to but with the addition that the seller has to procure transport insurance against the risk of loss of or damage to the goods during the carriage. The seller contracts with the insurer and pays the insurance premium.

Freight forwarder An agent who assists his or her exporter client in moving cargo to a foreign destination.

General Agreement on Tariffs and Trade (GATT) A multilateral trade treaty among governments embodying rights and obligations. The detailed rules set out in the agreement constitute a code that the parties to the agreement have agreed on to govern their trading relationships.

General license (export)   Government authorization to export without specific documentary approval.

Gross weight   Total weight of goods, packing, and container ready for shipment.

Handling charges   The forwarder's fee to his or her shipping client.

Import   To bring merchandise into a country from another country or overseas territory.

Import license   A government document that permits the importation of a product or material into a country where such licenses are necessary.

In bond   A term applied to the status of merchandise admitted provisionally into a country without payment of duties. See *Bonded warehouse*.

Inco terms   Indicate whether the buyer or the seller carries the risk, responsibility, liability, or costs at specific points during a transaction.

Inconvertibility   The inability to exchange the currency of one country for the currency of another.

Inherent vice   Defects or characteristics of a product that could lead to deterioration without outside influence. An insurance term. See *All-risks clause*.

Insurance certificate   A document issued by an insurance company, usually to the order of shipper, under a marine policy and in cover of a particular shipment of merchandise.

Invoice   See *Commercial invoice* and *Consular invoice*.

Irrevocable   Applied to letters of credit. A letter of credit that cannot be altered or canceled once it has been negotiated between the buyer and his or her bank.

Joint venture   A commercial or industrial enterprise in which principals of one company share control and ownership with principals of another.

L/C   Letter of credit.

Legal weight   The weight of goods plus any immediate wrappings that are sold along with the goods, for example, the weight of a tin can together with its contents. See *Net weight.*

Letter of credit (commercial)   Abbreviated L/C, a document issued by a bank at a buyer's request in favor of a seller promising to pay an agreed amount of money on receipt by the bank of certain documents within a specified time.

License   See *Exchange license, Export license, Import license,* and *Validated license.*

Licensing   The grant of technical assistance and service and/or the use of proprietary rights, such as a trademark or patent, in return for royalty payments.

MEA   Manufacturer's export agent. See *Export management company.*

Manufacturer's export agent (MEA)   See *Export management company.*

Marine insurance   An insurance that compensates the owner of goods transported overseas in the event of loss that cannot be legally recovered from the carrier. Also covers air shipments.

Marks   A set of letters, numbers, and/or geometric symbols, generally followed by the name of the port of destination, placed on packages for export for identification purposes.

Maturity date   The date on which a draft or acceptance becomes due for payment.

Most-favored-nation status   All countries having this designation receive equal treatment with respect to customs and tariffs.

Named point   See *Specific delivery point.*

Net weight   The weight of the goods alone without any immediate wrappings, for example, the weight of the contents of a tin can without the weight of the can. See *Legal weight*.

Nomenclature of the Customs Cooperation Council   This was known as the Brussels Classification Nomenclature prior to January 1, 1975. It is the customs tariff adhered to by most European countries and many other countries throughout the world, but not by the United States.

On-board bill of lading   A bill of lading in which a carrier acknowledges that goods have been placed on board a certain vessel.

Open cargo policy   Synonymous with *floating policy*. An insurance policy that binds the insurer automatically to protect with insurance all shipments made by the insured from the moment the shipment leaves the initial shipping point until delivered at destination. The insuring conditions include clauses naming such risks insured against as perils of the sea, fire, jettison, forcible theft, and barratry. See *Perils of the sea*, *Barratry*, and *All-risks clause*.

Order bill of lading   A bill of lading, negotiable, made out to the order of the shipper.

Packing list   A list that shows the number and kinds of packages being shipped; totals of gross, legal, and net weights of the packages; and marks and numbers on the packages. The list may be requested by an importer or may be required by an importing country to facilitate the clearance of goods through customs.

Perils of the sea   A marine insurance term used to designate heavy weather, stranding, lightning, collision, and seawater damage.

Piggybacking   The assigning of export marketing and distribution functions by one manufacturer to another.

Port marks   See *Marks*.

Pro forma invoice   An invoice forwarded by the seller of goods prior to shipment to advise the buyer of the weight and value of the goods.

Quota   The total quantity of a product or commodity that may be imported into a country without restriction or the penalty of additional duties or taxes.

Quotation   An offer to sell goods at a stated price and under stated terms.

Rate of exchange   The basis on which money of one country will be exchanged for that of another. Rates of exchange are established and quoted for foreign currencies on the basis of the demand, supply, and stability of the individual currencies. See *Exchange.*

Revocable   Applied to letters of credit. A letter of credit that can be altered or canceled by the buyer after he or she has opened it through his or her bank. See *Irrevocable.*

Royalty payment   The share of the product or profit paid by a licensee to his or her licenser. See *Licensing.*

S/D   See *Sight draft.*

S.I.T.C.   See *Standard International Trade Classification.*

Sales agent   See *Foreign sales representative.*

Sales representative   See *Foreign sales representative.*

Sanitary certificate   A certificate that attests to the purity or absence of disease or pests in the shipment of food products, plants, seeds, and live animals.

Schedule B   Refers to "Schedule B, Statistical Classification of Domestic and Foreign Commodities Exported from the United States." A seven-digit Schedule B number must be entered on the shipper's U.S. export declaration for every commodity shipped.

Shipper's Export Declaration   A form required by the U.S. Treasury Department and completed by a shipper showing the value, weight, consignee, destination, and so on of export shipments as well as Schedule B identification number.

Shipping documents   Commercial invoices, bills of lading, insurance certificates, consular invoices, and related documents.

Ship's manifest   A true list in writing of the individual shipments comprising the cargo of a vessel, signed by the captain.

Sight draft (S/D)   A draft so drawn as to be payable on presentation to the drawee or at a fixed or determinable date thereafter. See *Documents against acceptance* and *Documents against payment.*

Specific delivery point   A point in sales quotations that designates specifically where and within what geographic locale the goods will be delivered at the expense and responsibility of the seller, for example, F.A.S. named vessel at named port of export.

Standard Industrial Classification (SIC)   A numerical system developed by the U.S. government for the classification of commercial services and industrial products. Also classifies establishments by type of activity.

Standard International Trade Classification (SITC)   A numerical system developed by the United Nations to classify commodities used in international trade as an aid to reporting trade statistics.

Steamship conference   A group of vessel operators joined together for the purpose of establishing freight rates. A shipper may receive reduced rates if the shipper enters into a contract to ship on vessels of conference members only.

Stocking distributor   A distributor that maintains an inventory of goods of a manufacturer.

Straight bill of lading   A bill of lading, nonnegotiable, in which the goods are consigned directly to a named consignee.

Tare weight   The weight of packing and containers without the goods to be shipped.

Tariff   A schedule or system of duties imposed by a government on goods imported or exported; the rate of duty imposed in a tariff.

Tenor The time fixed or allowed for payment, as in "the tenor of a draft."

Time draft A draft drawn to mature at a certain fixed time after presentation or acceptance.

U.S. Standard Master A single business form with combined stencil that includes space for information required on many different export forms. Use of this form eliminates multiple typing.

Validated license A government document authorizing the export of commodities within the limitations set forth in the document.

Visa A signature of formal approval on a document. Obtained from consulates.

Wharfage Charge assessed by a carrier for the handling of incoming or outgoing ocean cargo.

Wholesale Merchandise, Packing, and Shipping Terms

Here are some wholesale merchandise, packing, and shipping terms from Via Trading's website (www.viatrading.com/wholesale/456/Glossary-of-Terms.html). They will help you to understand some common wholesale industry jargon.

Merchandise Terms

As-Is Refers to the selling conditions of certain merchandise. Buyer typically assumes all risks in purchasing such goods and that merchandise is sold with no guarantees or returns.

Closeout Selling the entire lot of remaining merchandise usually through a sale at reduced prices.

Customer return Item that has been purchased by a consumer and then returned to the store (or online store) for any number of reasons.

Defective   Items that have been put through a testing process and have been deemed defective or not working. Items may be visually defective or incomplete or be missing parts. Items also may be brand new but with a major quality control flaw, making them defective.

HBA   Health and beauty aids.

Label brands   Brands that are either private or specific store label brands (not national brands).

Manifest   A list of the items included in a load. Not all pallets or loads are manifested. If the load or pallet is manifested, you would be able to view a list of what would be in the load. Manifests are not 100 percent accurate, and some room for error should be expected. Manifests are typically generated by the department-store facility.

Master case   Master case goods are typically 100 percent new in the original manufacturer's packaging and are fully functional and complete. These goods have not been exposed for sale in any retail environment, and products can be considered 100 percent new and retail ready.

New overstock   Also often referred to as *closeouts*, tend to be goods that have typically never been merchandised or exposed for sale in a retail store. Such goods can materialize from importers, manufacturers, or distributors who are closing down or simply have excess goods in their warehouses that they need to move.

Preworn   Preworn condition typically refers to clothing and/or accessories that have previously been worn (used). They usually come without any kind of retail tags or labels.

Private/store label   Brands that are either private or specific store label brands (not national brands).

Refurbished   Items that have gone through a process to test and restore them to their original working condition. Often these items are repackaged in generic boxes and may not include all the items found in the original manufacturer's packaging.

Retail value The value of an item or load based on its original retail price in the store.

Seasonal goods Goods that are heavy in merchandise for a particular season such as Halloween, Easter, or Christmas.

Shelf pulls Typically overstocked goods that have been displayed for sale in a store or online but have never been purchased by a consumer.

Tested working Items that are typically in overstock, shelf-pull, or return condition but have been put through a testing process and have been deemed to be in working condition. These items may or may not come in original boxes, with or without all parts and accessories.

Wholesale The selling of goods in large quantities to retailers.

Packing Terms

Bin Large open cardboard box, which is similar to a *Gaylord*, but much shorter (approximately 24 inches in height).

Case pack/case lot Generally refers to loose items packed in a small case. Typically used for shipping smaller goods such as cosmetics, clothing, accessories, and so on. Case packs/lots usually have a predetermined unit count.

Gaylord Typically a large open cardboard box placed on top of a pallet and used to store or move large quantities or smaller loose items. They come in various sizes but are typically 48 inches by 48 inches by 48 inches.

Master case One hundred percent brand-new factory-sealed merchandise still in its original packaging.

Pallet Wooden (and sometimes plastic) structure used to support goods while in transit or being moved. Standard pallets are 40 inches by 48 inches and are typically moved using forklifts or pallet jacks.

Skid   Alternative term used to refer to a pallet.

Shipping Terms

Direct shipment   Refers to items that are shipped to a customer directly from a store's facility.

Drop shipping   An order that is placed with a vendor and shipped directly to an end consumer. (Brokers deal with drop shippers when they do not want to touch or warehouse the merchandise. They receive orders from their customers, then place a drop-ship order with a vendor, who then ships the merchandise directly to the broker's customer.) Drop-ship orders are typically shipped "blind," meaning with no trace of the vendor's name or address, to protect the broker.

LCL   Less than container load (an ocean shipment of less than a full container of pallets).

Lift-gate   A platform at the rear of a truck that is used to lower pallets to the ground/curb. A lift-gate is needed when you do not have a loading dock or forklift available at the delivery location.

Loading dock   A platform that usually matches the height of the floor of a truck that allows trucks to back up to the dock and permits easy and fast loading and unloading of the truck.

LTL   Less than load (a shipment of usually less than eight pallets).

OCL   Ocean container load (a full 20-, 40-, or 45-foot container of merchandise shipped via sea).

Index

About the Author

Jason A. Prescott, CEO of JP Communications, Inc., directs a network of global trade platforms used for sourcing products by millions of businesses and entrepreneurs. Anchored by TopTenWholesale.com and Manufacturer.com, over 2 million manufacturers, wholesalers, importers, retailers, and product resellers belong to the JP Communications, Inc., trade platforms. Mr. Prescott spearheaded the acquisition of Manufacturer.com from a group of Chinese nationals and foreign investors in 2009. JP Communications, Inc., operates in China under Hangzhou Flat World Sourcing, Ltd.

Mr. Prescott is a pioneer in business-to-business online trade platforms. He has given presentations at Search Engine Strategies, SIPPA, SANDIOS, ASD Trade Shows (Strategies to Sell Chain Stores), and the San Diego Software Council. Mr. Prescott also has provided consulting and educational seminars in China for entrepreneurs wishing to invest in the U.S. market and has given seminars in China to various government entities. He has consulted with hundreds of Chinese, South American, Mexican, and Central American factories on international export strategies. In addition, Mr. Prescott authored one of the first search marketing courses for the Search Engine Marketing Professionals Organization and was on SEMPO's Education Committee.

Besides presentations and consulting, Mr. Prescott has authored articles on business and technology appearing in B2B Online, OMMA, IMediaConnection, *CEO Magazine*, and Entrepreneur Online. He has been cited in *Inc Magazine*, *Business Week*, and Forbes Online. JP Communications' trade platforms are partnered with industry trade-show giants: SOURCING at MAGIC, ASD, the Off Price Show, Internet Retailer, and the National Hardware Show.

When it comes to accomplishments, Mr. Prescott was named as U.S. investment advisor to the city of Jiaozhou, China, in 2011. JP Communications, Inc., was awarded the first international broker agreement by the ASD Trade Show in 2011 as a company from the United States that successfully brought in several of China's most prominent electronics manufacturers and exporters. Mr. Prescott was also chosen by the China Chamber of Commerce for Import and Export of Textile to lead its post-Sourcing at MAGIC trade-show delegation on a tour of Los Angeles, the Fashion Institute of Design and Merchandising (FIDM), and sourcing events. He took part in the Los Angeles mayor's delegation to China in 2011 to promote bilateral trade and investment in the high-tech/energy sector. Mr. Prescott was chosen as the online sourcing B2B partner of SOURCING at MAGIC, ASD, National Hardware Show, Off Price Show, and Internet Retailer. Lastly, Mr. Prescott has successfully closed grants and government funding from Beijing.

Mr. Prescott's trade platforms have received awards as well. Recently, Inc.com included TopTenWholesale as one of the top 12 "Google Killers" in a slide presentation that included popular search engines such as Yahoo and Ask and innovative engines such as Hakia and Powerset. Additionally, TopTenWholesale was given a "Number 1 in Fast Growth" award (2008) by bizSanDiego and a "Top 20 for Technology" award sponsored by *San Diego Business Journal*.

Mr. Prescott was named in the "Top 40 Entrepreneurs under 40" roster in 2007 by San Diego's *Metropolitan Magazine*. He was recognized for "Outstanding Emerging Business of the Year" (San Diego Chamber of Commerce) and as "People to Watch in CA" (*San Diego Union-Tribune*).

Mr. Prescott is a graduate of Western Connecticut State University, Law Administration and Marketing. He currently resides in Los Angeles.

About the Writer and Research Assistant

Tara Gladstone is a freelance writer and editor. She provides editorial services for both fiction and nonfiction titles. Prior to working as a freelance writer, Tara worked for Edelman as a senior account executive, providing editorial services for brands such as eBay and Hewlett-

Packard. Before joining Edelman, she worked for Waterside Productions, the world's leading literary agency for computer and technical books. Tara's media and editorial experience also includes in-house work at DanceMedia, LCC, where she wrote for various online and offline publications. She secured a BA from the University of Colorado at Boulder and holds an MA in public relations and press office communications from the Autonomous University of Barcelona. She currently resides in Barcelona, Spain.